The *Beatrix Potter* Toys and Designs Book

The *Beatrix Potter*™ Toys and Designs Book

Eden Toys, Anne Wilkinson,
Pat Menchini, Jennie Walters
and Amanda Clifford

Photography by Ian O'Leary

CLAREMONT/WARNE

Acknowledgements
The authors and publishers would like to thank the
following for their assistance:

Laura Ashley for the armchair, *Campbell Marson* for
the flooring and *Mothercare* for the Moses basket.
Coats Patons Craft Ltd for embroidery threads, knitting
yarns and embroidery fabrics and *Atlascraft* of
Nottingham for canvas, rug wool and making up of the
rug. *Hanne McDonald* for her exquisite cross-stitch
embroidery and *Joyce Turner* and *Joan Cowper* for
knitting the designs. *Noah Akinci*, *Guy McLean* and
Alice O'Leary and her dog, *Ruby*, for being such good
models. *Ian Garlick* for photographic assistance and
Marian Price, stylist.

(Beatrix Potter's Toys and Designs Book)

CLAREMONT BOOKS
in association with Frederick Warne

Published by the Penguin Group
27 Wright's Lane, London W8 5TZ, England
Penguin Books USA Inc., 375 Hudson Street, New York, New York 10014, USA
Penguin Books Australia Ltd, Ringwood, Victoria, Australia
Penguin Books Canada Ltd, 10 Alcorn Avenue, Toronto, Ontario, Canada M4V 3B2
Penguin Books (NZ) Ltd, 182-190 Wairau Road, Auckland 10, New Zealand

Penguin Books Ltd, Registered Offices: Harmondsworth, Middlesex, England

Claremont Books, an imprint of the Godfrey Cave Group, 42 Bloomsbury Street, London WC1B 3QJ

First published 1992 as *Toys and Designs from the World of Beatrix Potter* by Frederick Warne
This edition first published 1995
1 3 5 7 9 10 8 6 4 2

Text copyright © Frederick Warne & Co., 1992
Photographs copyright © Ian O'Leary, 1992
Original copyright in Beatrix Potter's original illustrations included in this volume
© Frederick Warne & Co., 1902, 1904, 1905, 1906, 1907, 1908, 1909, 1910, 1930

New reproductions of Beatrix Potter's book illustrations copyright © Frederick Warne & Co., 1987

ISBN 1 85471 6832

Compiled by Naia Bray-Moffatt
Designed by Amanda Clifford
Typeset by Goodfellow & Egan, Cambridge

Printed and bound in Great Britain by
BPC Hazell Books Ltd
A member of
The British Printing Company Ltd

CONTENTS

INTRODUCTION   8

TOYS
By Eden Toys, Inc.

GENERAL INSTRUCTIONS   12

SOFT TOYS   17
Peter Rabbit, Mrs Rabbit and Benjamin Bunny   18
Jemima Puddle-duck   29

PUPPETS   36
Peter Rabbit Velour Glove Puppet   38
Peter Rabbit Fur-fabric Hand Puppet with Legs   40

BEAN BAGS   47
Peter Rabbit   47
Hunca Munca   48

SMALL SOFT TOYS AND FINGER PUPPETS   53
Peter Rabbit, Jemima Puddle-duck and Mouse   53

HAND-PAINTED FABRIC TOYS
By Anne Wilkinson

PETER RABBIT BALL   61

POCKET TOYS WITH BAG   65

POCKET TOY MOBILE   73

PETER RABBIT DRAWSTRING BAG   75

JEMIMA PUDDLE-DUCK POCKET   76

KNITTING AND NEEDLEPOINT
By Pat Menchini

HUNCA MUNCA SAMPLER	81
MRS TITTLEMOUSE SEMI-CIRCULAR TUFTED RUG	90
KNITTED TRIANGULAR SHAWL	95
JEMIMA PUDDLE-DUCK PRAM COVER	99
CROSS-STITCH BABIES' BIBS	101

DECORATING FURNITURE
By Jennie Walters and designs by Amanda Clifford

GENERAL INSTRUCTIONS	106
STENCILLING	109
DÉCOUPAGE	119
PETER RABBIT AND FRIENDS WOODEN CUT-OUTS	121

'At present I intend to make dolls; I think I could make him [Peter] stand on his legs if he had some lead bullets in his feet!'

INTRODUCTION

For many children, their first introduction to Peter Rabbit and his friends will not have been through the little books themselves, but through the seemingly endless commercial products available, ranging from babies' bottles and soft toys to bedlinen and wallpapers. This commercial activity is not, as might be imagined, a recent development. In fact, toys and other products sporting designs copied from Beatrix Potter's illustrations began to appear almost from the moment her books went on sale and caught the public's imagination. Peter Rabbit, hero of the first book, in his little blue jacket with brass buttons, has always been especially popular and it was Beatrix Potter herself who designed and made the first Peter Rabbit doll, registering it at the Patent Office in London as early as 1903, only a year after *The Tale of Peter Rabbit* was published. Other dolls based on her characters but not designed by Beatrix also quickly came on to the market; Mr Potter purchased a squirrel he saw displayed in the Burlington Arcade labelled 'Nutkin' shortly after *The Tale of Squirrel Nutkin* was published, proving, if proof were needed, the tremendous popularity of the animal world Beatrix had created.

The Peter Rabbit doll made by Beatrix in 1903

The transformation of Peter Rabbit and friends from the page into three-dimensional figures and designs for commercial products was a development that Beatrix found fascinating and one in which she became very involved. After designing the Peter Rabbit doll, she was keen to begin making a mouse threading a rug needle, but became sidetracked by an acquaintance into designing a nursery-wall frieze featuring Peter Rabbit and

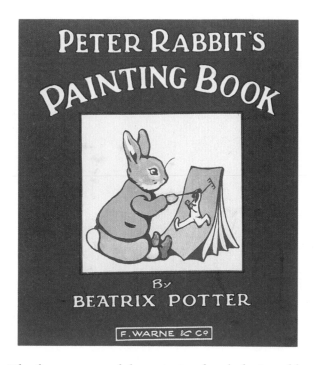

The front cover of the painting book designed by Beatrix and published in 1911

designs. Similarly, the toys and designs included in this book are intended to be fun to make as well as fun for children to play and live with. The contributors found themselves as brimming with ideas as Beatrix Potter herself and so, whether you want to create a complete Beatrix Potter nursery or just make individual items, perhaps as presents for friends, there are lots of toys and designs to choose from. You may even find you are inspired to create your own designs!

Mr McGregor: 'We have done them flat, like stencil colours; they are less frightful than might have been expected, and Mr. McGregor is magnificent on the frieze.' At the same time she devised a Peter Rabbit game, and later was encouraged to design a Peter Rabbit painting book. On the whole, however, she needed little prompting and ideas for new projects were always forthcoming. Even when she had finished writing the books and was concentrating on sheep farming in the Lake District she would write to her editor with comments and new suggestions: 'The nursery articles mentioned in your letter this morning sound quite a good idea. I wonder whether there is a crawling rug on the market? with cut-out applique figures.'

Clearly, Beatrix enjoyed both thinking of new ideas for developing her Peter Rabbit books and actually making the

Beatrix with her tame rabbit, Benjamin, in September 1891

9

TOYS

As Beatrix Potter discovered when she was making
her Peter Rabbit doll nearly 100 years ago,
making your own toys is both great fun and very
rewarding: 'I am cutting calico patterns of Peter.
I have not got it right yet, but the expression
is going to be lovely; especially the whiskers –
(pulled out of a brush!).'
The designs included here do not require you to be
an expert in toy-making. There are a wide range of
characters and toys to choose from involving
different craft techniques to give as much variety as
possible. For a baby, you could make the fabric
painted animal mobile to hang over the cot, or the
soft-toy ball for a very young child; an older child
might like to play with the hand and finger
puppets, or to collect the family of
soft-toy rabbits.

GENERAL INSTRUCTIONS

SOFT TOYS

Choosing your material

Try to buy high quality fur fabric; the finished result will look much better and wear longer. When you have decided which toy you want to make, it is a good idea to look at the relevant original Beatrix Potter book, as well as the photograph of the toy in this book, to help you choose the right colour of material to buy.

Preparing the patterns

The patterns, found at the end of each project, are full size, but you need to allow an extra 5 mm (¼ in) all round for the seams. Use carbon paper to trace the pattern pieces on to thick card. Card templates are much easier to trace around than paper patterns and will last longer, so they can be used many times.

When you have cut out all the templates you need, mark them to indicate the direction of the nap or pile.

Cutting the fabric

It is easiest to use small, sharp scissors, especially for cutting fur fabric. Cut only the back of the fabric and not the pile so that the pile can mask the seams on the finished toy.

Remember to check that the pile or nap is running in the right direction, particularly when cutting out folded fabric.

Sewing

Sew all the pattern pieces with the right sides together, unless otherwise instructed.

As you are making the toy, clip the curves and corners, and trim seams where necessary.

Turning

Use a blunt tool for turning material right side out, such as a small screwdriver or the handle of a brush or spoon. Scissors are too sharp and will push through the fabric.

Useful stitches

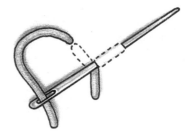

The Y stitch   To sew the nose, push the needle through from the base of the head to the tip of the nose. Sew three small stitches as shown above to form a Y shape.

French knot   Push the needle through the fabric and wrap the thread round the needle two or three times. Tighten the twists, turn the needle and insert it back into the fabric. Pull tight.

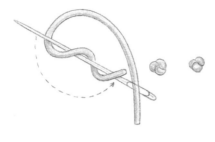

Making the whiskers

1. For sewing whiskers with two strands on each side, thread your needle with a single strand of fishing line. If you want whiskers with 4 strands on each side, thread your needle with double strands and even up the ends of fishing line before applying.

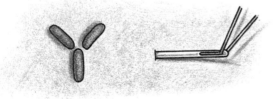

2. Insert the needle horizontally into the head about 3 cm (1 in) to the side of the nose.

3. Making sure it is completely straight, push the needle through the head, bringing it up the same distance away from the nose on the other side, leaving approximately 5 cm (2 in) of line protruding from the first side.

4. Tie a knot in the line, pulling it tightly against the surface of the material.

5. Reinsert the needle next to the knot, again keeping it as straight as possible, and pull it out as close to the whiskers on the first side as possible.
6. Pull the line through tightly and trim the ends.
7. Repeat this process for the whiskers on the other side.

Mice making coats, from The Tailor of Gloucester

PAINTED FABRIC TOYS

Preparing the patterns
Again, the patterns found at the end of each project are full size. They include a 5 mm (¼ in) seam allowance.

Materials
Fabric Paints The best fabric paints to use are Dylon 'Color Fun', which are available in a wide range of colours. The instructions in this chapter replace those on the label of the jars.
Material White cotton calico is ideal for making the toys. It is important that the material is thin enough to be able to trace the patterns from the book directly on to the fabric.

Tracing the image on to fabric
Practise using the superfine fabric-marking pen on a spare piece of fabric first. If the pen is new and full of ink, you need a fairly light even touch or the line may bleed in places. When you feel confident, tape your fabric over the image

you require and trace it.

It is best to draw the outline (the outside edge of the pattern piece) in pencil so that it does not show on the finished article. The rest of the drawing should be done in the superfine pen. Remember, you are going to paint the drawing, so if it bleeds a bit here and there, it can be covered up. When you have completed your tracing, place it on a folded sheet of spare fabric to absorb excess moisture, and you are ready to paint.

Painting the fabric
Again, it is best to practise first. You may find that you like to use the paint straight from the pot, or you may find it easier to mix it with a little water. It is best to paint an undercoat, let it dry, then work on that. Practise on one or two simple images and allow yourself plenty of time – you need time and patience!

In the case of shaped pieces, such as the pocket toys, paint to the edge of the inside line but not to the edge of the shape. It is best to leave a blank hem so you can see the shape when sewing round.

When your painting is dry, iron on the wrong side with a very hot iron before cutting out.

You can put on the finishing touches in pen and paint when the article has been turned and stuffed. This is the most satisfying part of the whole operation. You will achieve effects that are impossible in commercially produced printed products, so each item you make will be a unique work of art.

Mixing the colours
When painting the characters' clothes, use

14

the blue and pink straight from the pot as an undercoat, then mix it with white to add touches of light. If you want to keep it simple, use just the flat colour, but it adds life and charm to create tonal charges.

You need to mix a special colour for the brown of the fur in Peter, Tom and Mrs Tittlemouse, and it is a good idea to make quite a large quantity in a separate jar. Mix the dark brown, white and yellow until you have the colour you feel is right. Mix well with a little water.

It is easy to create different shades and tones of green by mixing the jade with blue, with yellow and with white.

The yellow works best mixed with a little white.

The red can be mixed with a little white to use on the geranium and radishes.

Fabric painting is an art, like any other form of painting. You will find your own way of doing it. Have patience and your confidence will grow!

You will want a Brush and 5 Paints ——
Antwerp Blue
Crimson Lake
Gamboge
Sap Green and
Burnt Sienna

You can mix Blue with the Sienna to make dark Brown. Don't put the Brush in your mouth. If you do, you will be ill, like Peter.

Instructions for mixing colours from The Peter Rabbit Painting Book

SOFT TOYS

There are few things that children love more than a soft toy they can hug and which won't break even with a lot of wear and tear. What more perfect a present for a child than a toy which represents one of their favourite characters. You can make these lovely soft toys using either velour or a fur fabric and then make the clothes to complete the character.

From The Tale of Peter Rabbit

PETER RABBIT, MRS RABBIT AND BENJAMIN BUNNY

Measure: 30 cm (12 in)

Peter Rabbit and Benjamin Bunny

YOU WILL NEED

The body
½ metre (½ yd) of tan velour or fur fabric
    5–10 mm (¼ in) pile height
23 cm (¼ yd) white velour or fur fabric
11½ cm (⅛ yd) white fur fabric,
    10–20 mm (½ in) pile height
2 14-mm (½-in) black or brown safety
    eyes or buttons
dark brown embroidery thread

thick clear fishing line for whiskers
polyester stuffing

Peter's and Benjamin's jacket
corduroy, velveteen or velour – blue for
    Peter, brown for Benjamin
2 or 3 10-mm (¼-in) brass buttons

Radish
10 × 10 cm (4 × 4 in) red or pink felt
scrap of green felt or green silk

Benjamin's hat
Red silk flower for pompon
23 cm (¼ yd) green knitted fabric

Benjamin's handkerchief
15 × 15 cm (6 × 6 in) red cotton fabric

Mrs Rabbit's dress
23 cm (¼ yd) blue print cotton
1 m (1 yd) 2½-cm (1-in) wide elastic

Mrs Rabbit's apron
12 cm (⅛ yd) white cotton fabric
1 m (1 yd) 2½-cm (1-in) white bias
    binding

Mrs Rabbit's shawl
*23 cm (¼ yd) pink knitted fabric or a
pink–and–blue paisley handkerchief*

TO MAKE

1. Sew the two ear-liners to the two outer ear pieces, leaving the straight edge open. Turn right side out.
2. Fold the bottom of the ears in at either side so that they meet in the middle to create an ear shape, and tack (baste) in position.

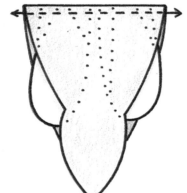

Diagram A

3. Place the front head on top of the back head with edges matching. Fit the ears, ear-liners facing up, between the two head pieces, so that the straight edges fit the notches, as shown in diagram A. Pin the straight edges together and then sew.
4. Pin one of the side head pieces to the front head, matching points B, C and D. Starting from B, tack (baste) the two pieces together until you come to the bottom of the back head E. Do the same with the other side head piece, but leave a gap of 5 cm (2 in) at the bottom so that it will be easier to sew the head on to the body later. Now tack (baste) together the two side head pieces from B to A to complete the head shape before sewing

properly.
5. If using safety eyes, pierce tiny holes at the eye positions with the end of a small pair of sharp scissors. Insert the safety eyes through the holes and secure on the reverse with the metal washers provided. If using buttons, sew to the head after it has been stuffed.
6. Embroider the nose, using the Y stitch (see page 12). Each stitch should measure 15 mm (⅝ in).
7. Sew the darts closed on each side of the head.
8. Place the two front body pieces together and sew the seam A–B.
9. Place the two inside arms on either side of the front body, matching the notches (D), and sew together. Do the same with the inside legs, but sew only as far as E.
10. Match the side bodies to the front body and sew together. Leave the back open.
11. Pin the bottom to the body, matching points A at the front and J and the sides. Sew all round.
12. Sew the two tail pieces together, leaving the wedge shape open. Turn the tail right side out. Fold it in half and sew it between H and I on the back body.
13. To sew the head on to the body, match notch C on the front body to the seam running down the middle of the face and, with right sides together, sew all the way round the neck. Now sew up the gap left at the back of the head.
14. Sew up the back, leaving F to G open. Turn the rabbit right side out and stuff. Sew the back opening closed by hand.

Peter's and Benjamin's jacket
1. Hem across the top and bottom of the

Peter trying on his jacket, from The Tale of Benjamin Bunny

back jacket.

2. Place the front jacket pieces on the back jacket, and sew along the top sleeves of both arms.

3. Hem round the wrists.

4. Sew the darts closed in the front jacket pieces. Then, matching the notches, sew the interfacing to the front jacket pieces. Sew the sides of the jacket closed.

5. Turn the jacket right side out and, starting from the shoulder seam, top-stitch about 3 mm (⅛ in) in from the edge down the front to the side seam.

6. Fold the top of the front jacket pieces down approx. 2½ cm (1 in) from the shoulder to make a lapel and top-stitch down (see diagram B).

7. Sew the buttons on the right side of the jacket.

Peter's radish

1. Fold the leaf or leaves in half, match the straight edge to the top notch of the radish and pin.

2. Fold the radish in half over the leaves so that the right sides are together and sew round the radish, leaving an opening at one side to turn.

3. Turn the radish right side out and stuff (see diagram C).

4. Hand-sew the opening closed.

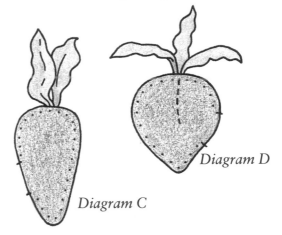

Diagram D

Diagram C

Benjamin's radish

1. Fold the leaves in half.

2. Sew closed the darts in the radish. Place the two radish halves with right sides together, and put the folded leaves between them, pointing down, where the darts meet. Sew the two sides together, leaving an opening at the side to turn.

3. Turn the radish right side out and stuff (see diagram D).

4. Hand-sew the opening closed.

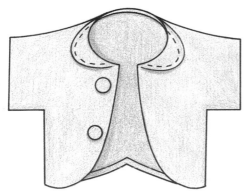

Diagram B

Benjamin's hat

1. Pleat the top hat around the edge by sewing together the pairs of notches.
2. Gather together the folds of material at the large opening in the middle of the hat, and sew closed.
3. Tack (baste) round the ear openings on the top and bottom hat to prevent the knitted material unravelling.
4. Match up the ear openings and sew the bottom hat to the top hat.
5. Turn the hat right side out through the ear opening, and sew the silk flower to the top hat at the middle seam.

Benjamin's handkerchief

Turn the edges down 5 mm (¼ in) on all sides and hem round.

Mrs Rabbit's dress

1. Pin the front to the back and sew along the sleeve top to the neck (A–B) on one side. Do the same with the other side, but

Frontispiece for The Tale of Benjamin Bunny

'Now run along, and don't get into mischief. I am going out.' From The Tale of Peter Rabbit

leave a gap of approx. 3 cm (1½ in) from the neck.
2. Hem round the neck and wrists. Sew the elastic on top of the hem around the neck and wrists. Sew the top sleeve closed.
3. Sew along the sleeve bottoms C–D, then sew the sides together D–E.
4. Turn up the bottom of the dress approx. 5 mm (¼ in) and hem all the way round, including the opening for the tail.

Mrs Rabbit's apron

1. Hem 5 mm (¼ in) round the three sides of the apron.
2. Gather the top of the apron to measure 7 cm (2¾ in). Fold the bias tape in half lengthways and sew it along the top of the apron, leaving approximately 25 cm (10 in) on either side of the apron to tie round the waist.

Mrs Rabbit's shawl

Hem along the top edge of the shawl. Fray the other two sides to make a fringe.

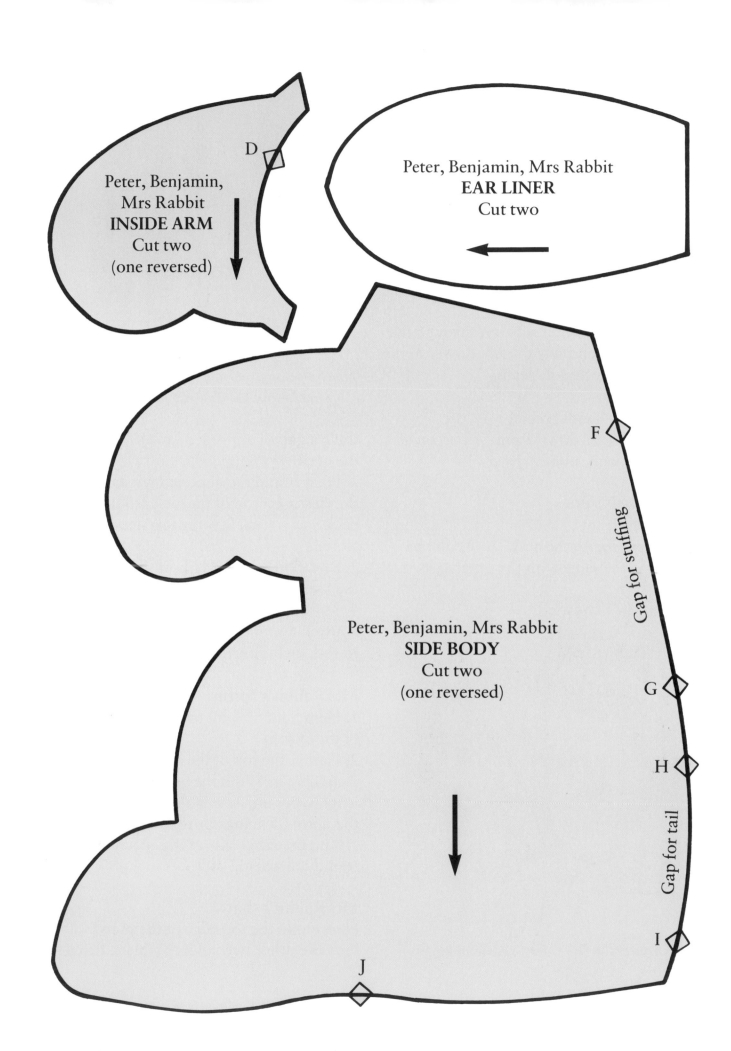

Peter, Benjamin,
Mrs Rabbit
INSIDE ARM
Cut two
(one reversed)

D

Peter, Benjamin, Mrs Rabbit
EAR LINER
Cut two

Peter, Benjamin, Mrs Rabbit
SIDE BODY
Cut two
(one reversed)

F

Gap for stuffing

G

H

Gap for tail

I

J

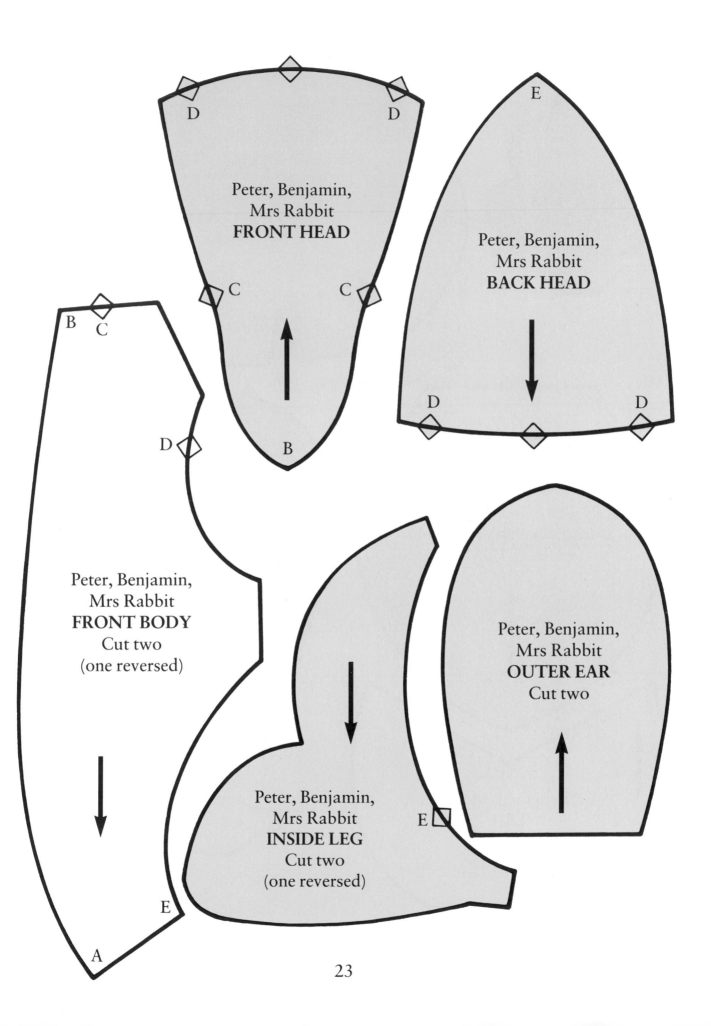

Peter, Benjamin,
Mrs Rabbit
FRONT HEAD

Peter, Benjamin,
Mrs Rabbit
BACK HEAD

Peter, Benjamin,
Mrs Rabbit
FRONT BODY
Cut two
(one reversed)

Peter, Benjamin,
Mrs Rabbit
OUTER EAR
Cut two

Peter, Benjamin,
Mrs Rabbit
INSIDE LEG
Cut two
(one reversed)

23

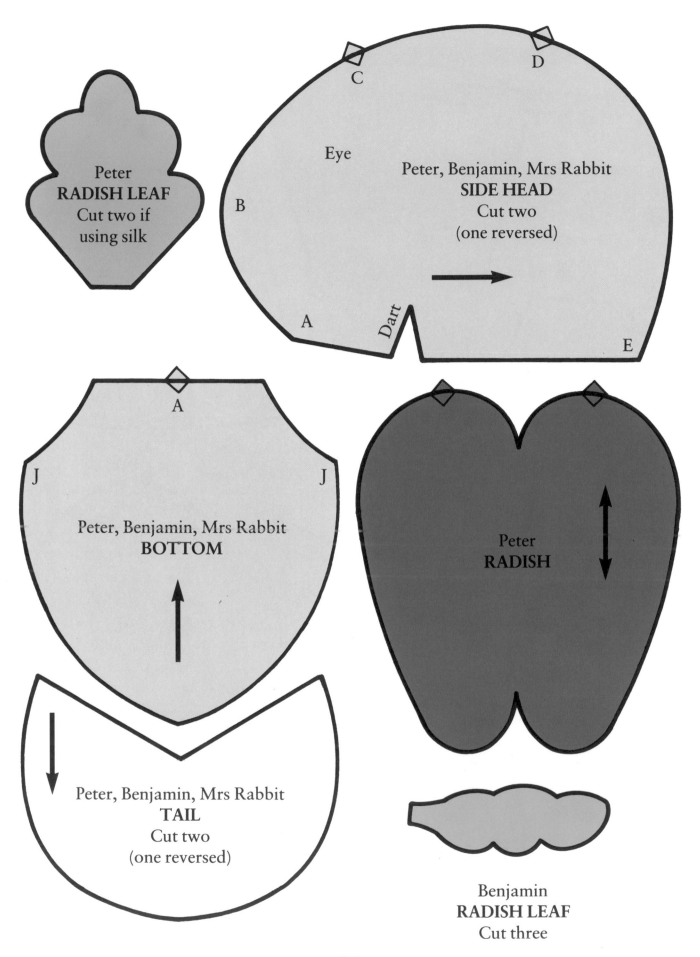

Peter
RADISH LEAF
Cut two if
using silk

Eye

Peter, Benjamin, Mrs Rabbit
SIDE HEAD
Cut two
(one reversed)

B

A

C

D

Dart

E

A

J

J

Peter, Benjamin, Mrs Rabbit
BOTTOM

Peter
RADISH

Peter, Benjamin, Mrs Rabbit
TAIL
Cut two
(one reversed)

Benjamin
RADISH LEAF
Cut three

24

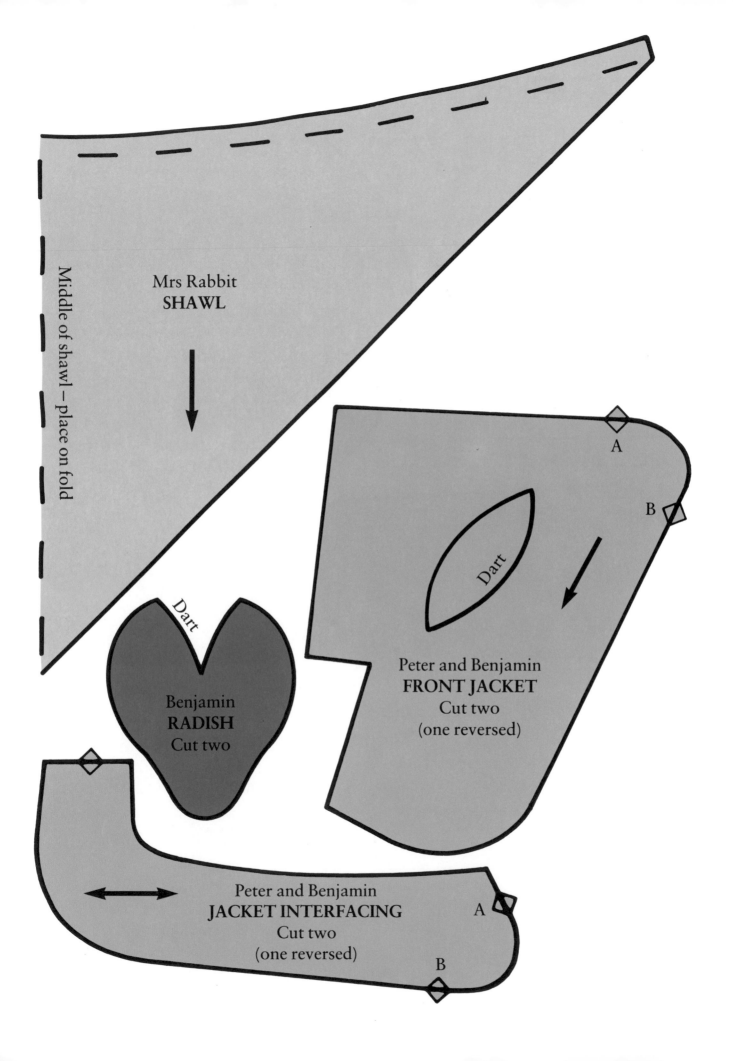

Middle of shawl – place on fold

Mrs Rabbit
SHAWL

Dart

Peter and Benjamin
FRONT JACKET
Cut two
(one reversed)

A

B

Dart

Benjamin
RADISH
Cut two

Peter and Benjamin
JACKET INTERFACING
Cut two
(one reversed)

A

B

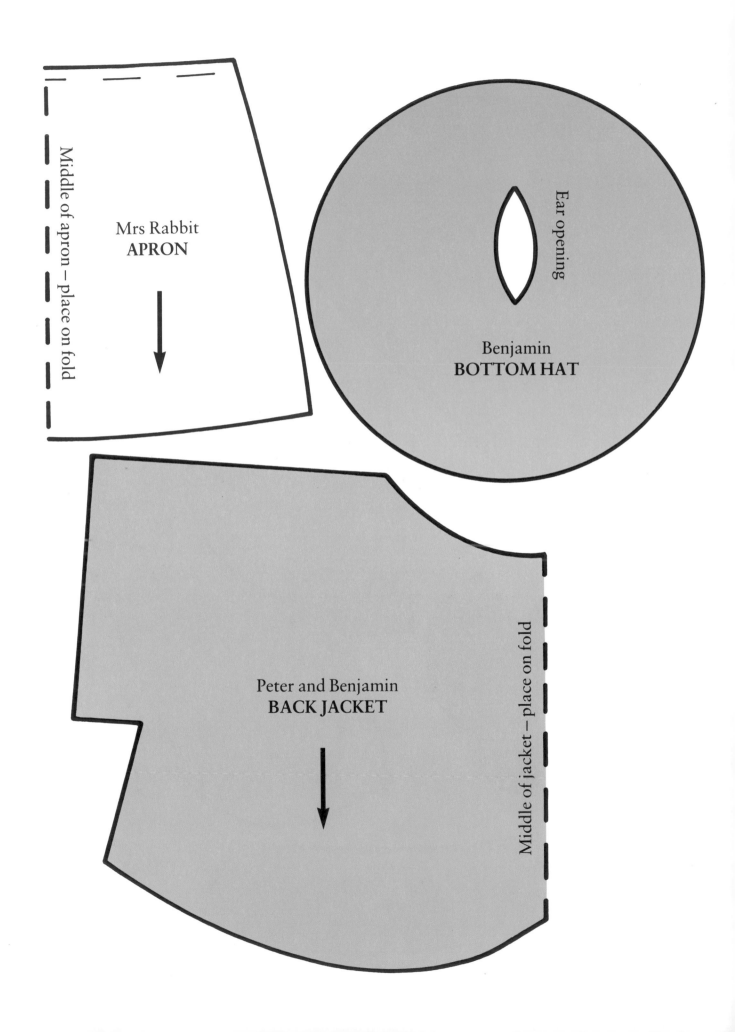

Middle of apron – place on fold

Mrs Rabbit
APRON

Ear opening

Benjamin
BOTTOM HAT

Peter and Benjamin
BACK JACKET

Middle of jacket – place on fold

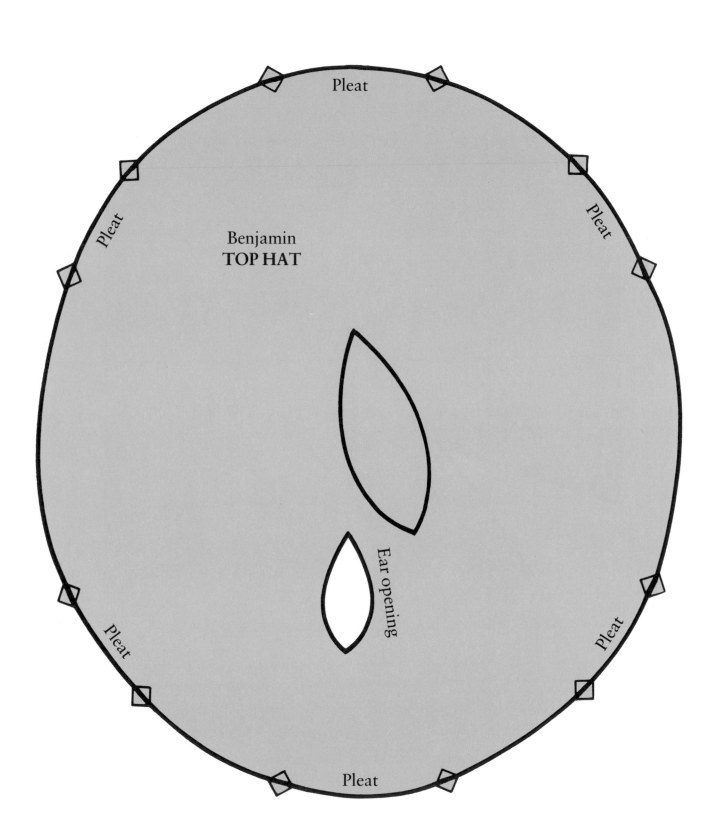

Benjamin
TOP HAT

Pleat

Pleat

Pleat

Pleat

Pleat

Pleat

Pleat

Pleat

Ear opening

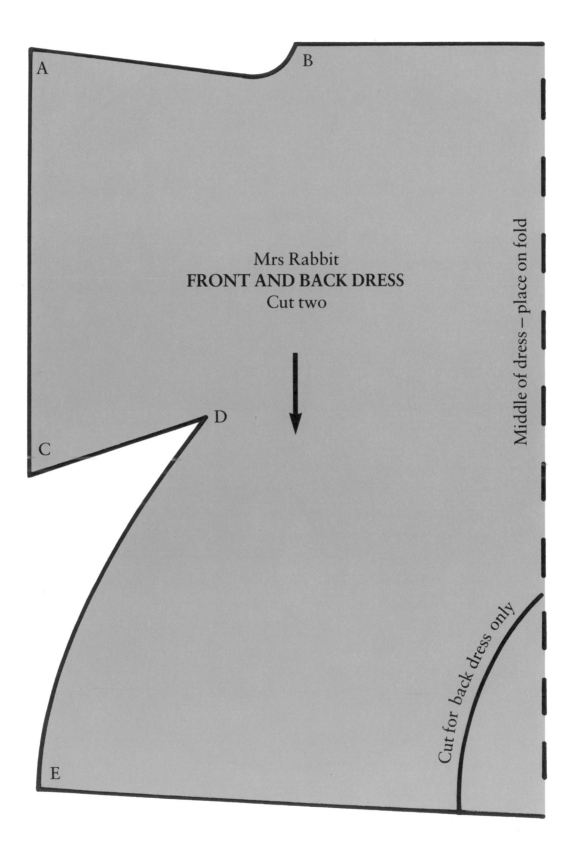

Mrs Rabbit
FRONT AND BACK DRESS
Cut two

A

B

C

D

E

Middle of dress – place on fold

Cut for back dress only

JEMIMA PUDDLE-DUCK

Measures: 25 cm (10 in)

Jemima Puddle-duck

YOU WILL NEED

*½ m (½ yd) white velour or fur fabric
    with 5–10 mm (¼ in) pile height
23 cm (¼ yd) yellow velour or felt
23 cm (¼ yd) blue cotton or blend fabric
23 cm (¼ yd) patchwork or floral print
    cotton
1 m (1 yd) blue bias binding, 2½ cm (1 in)
    wide to match bonnet
blue embroidery thread (for eyes for
    velour version) or*

*2 10-mm (¼-in) blue or black safety eyes
    (for fabric version)
polyester stuffing*

TO MAKE

1. Sew together the sides of the top beak and bottom beak, leaving the slit in the bottom beak open.
2. Leaving the straight edge open, sew each pair of feet together. Turn right side out and slightly stuff the feet. Then top-stitch two web lines about 2 cm (¾ in) long on both feet (diagram A).

Diagram A

3. Follow step 2 for the wings, omitting the web lines!
4. Push the wings through the slit on each side body piece. Sew the wings on from the wrong side of the fabric (see diagram B).

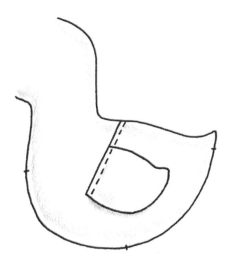

Diagram B

5. Place the front stomach on the back stomach. Fit the feet between these two pieces at the notches, and sew across the seam (see diagram C).

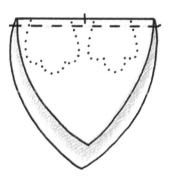

Diagram C

6. Sew the centre head to the side body head from A on the face to B at the back of the head on both sides (see diagram D).

From The Tale of Jemima Puddle-duck

7. If using safety eyes, pierce tiny holes at the eye positions with the end of a small pair of sharp scissors. Insert the safety eyes through the holes and secure on the reverse with the metal washers provided. If using buttons, sew to the head after it has been stuffed.

8. To sew the beak to the head, start from the slit in the bottom beak and the bottom of the face. When you have sewn all the way round, close the slit in the beak and sew the chin and front neck closed down to C on the chest (see diagram E).

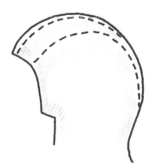

Diagram D

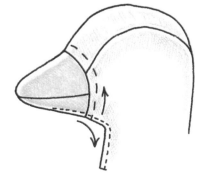

Diagram E

9. Sew the stomach to both sides of the body, starting at C. Leave an opening of approx. 5 cm (2 in) on one side near the tail for turning and stuffing (see diagram F).

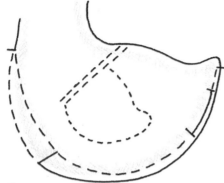

Diagram F

10. Turn the toy right side out and stuff. Close the opening by hand.

'She was wearing a shawl and a poke bonnet.'

Jemima's bonnet
1. Sew the brim pieces together along the outside edge. Turn the brim right side out and top-stitch 3 mm (⅛ in) from the edge.
2. Sew closed the darts at the back of the main hat piece. Gather in the bottom edge of the hat so it measures 8½ cm (3¾ in). Do the same round the outer edge of the hat, using the inside edge of the brim as a guide for how much you should gather.
3. Sew the brim to the outer edge of the bonnet.
4. Fold the bias binding in half lengthways and sew to the bottom back edge of the hat, leaving 10 cm (4 in) on each side for tying.

Jemima's shawl
Hem round all sides of the shawl 3 mm (⅛ in).

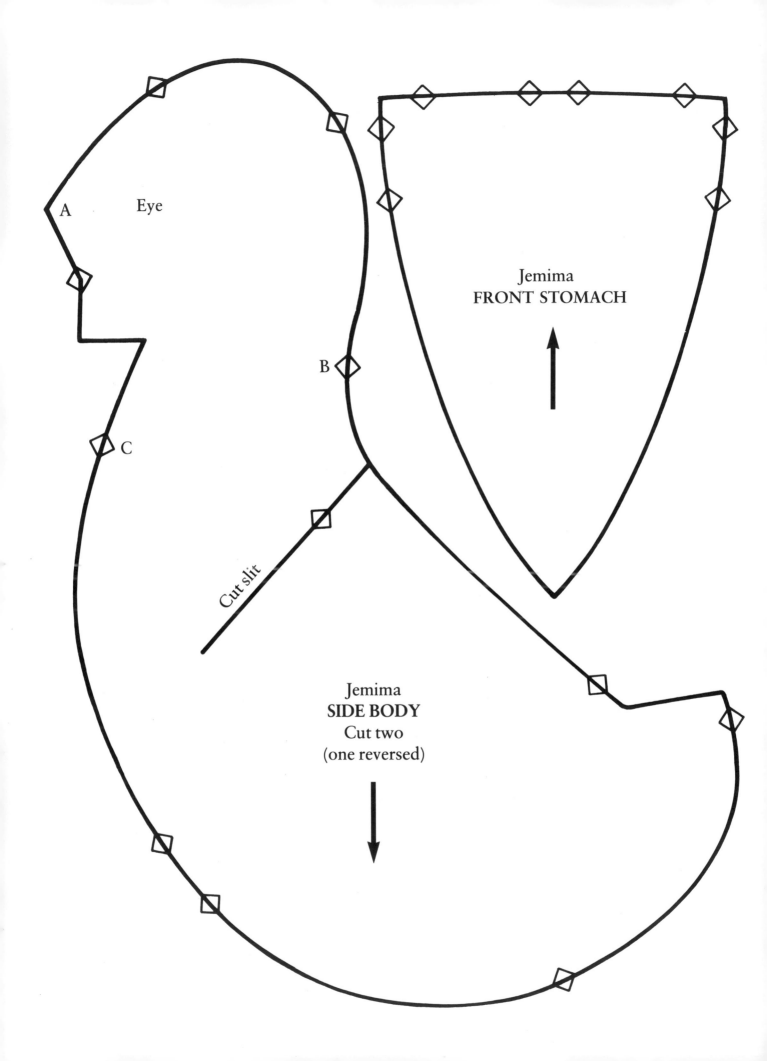

A

Eye

B

C

Jemima
FRONT STOMACH

Cut slit

Jemima
SIDE BODY
Cut two
(one reversed)

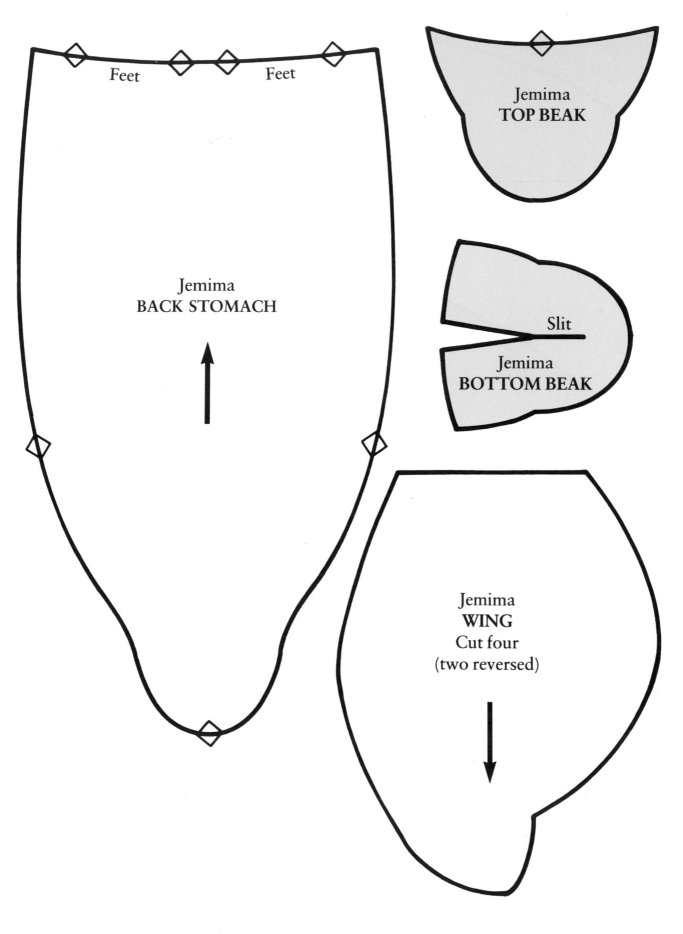

Feet   Feet

Jemima
TOP BEAK

Jemima
BACK STOMACH

Slit

Jemima
BOTTOM BEAK

Jemima
WING
Cut four
(two reversed)

33

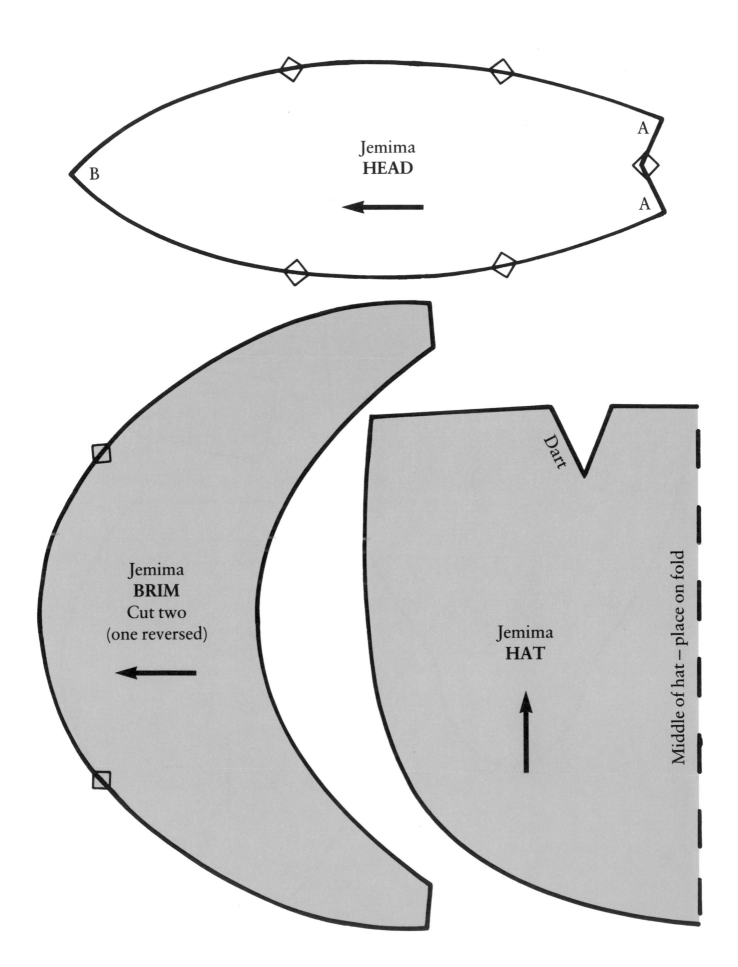

Jemima
HEAD

B

A

A

Jemima
BRIM
Cut two
(one reversed)

Dart

Jemima
HAT

Middle of hat – place on fold

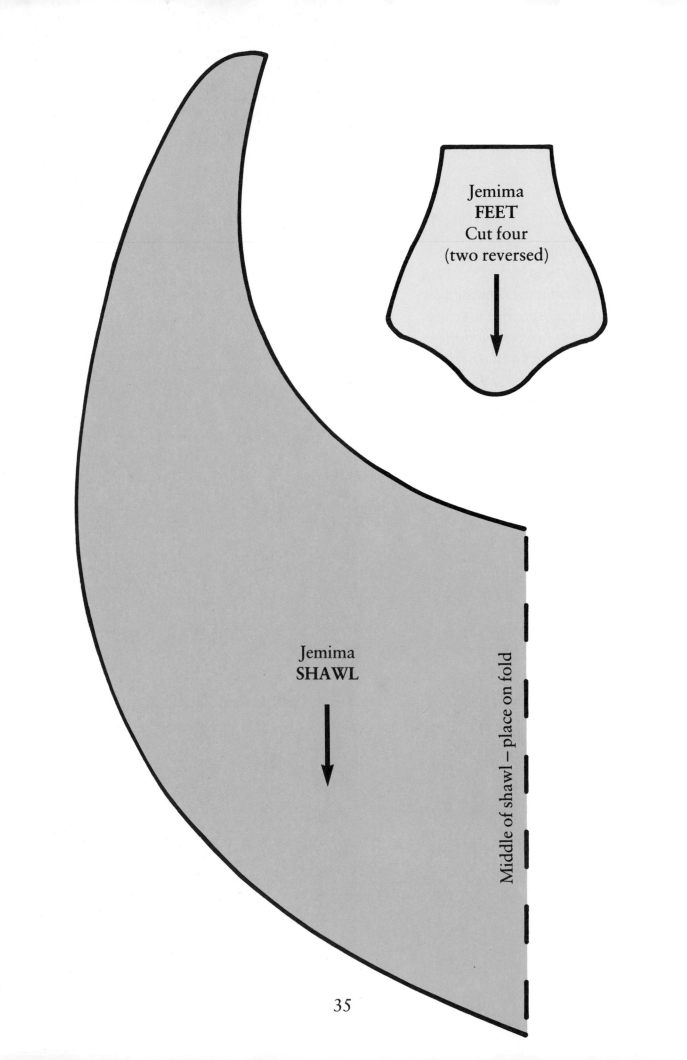

Jemima
FEET
Cut four
(two reversed)

Jemima
SHAWL

Middle of shawl – place on fold

PUPPETS

Children will love these Peter Rabbit puppets, which they can make come alive with their hands. They are quite simple to make and you can choose between a floppy velour glove puppet and a cuddly fur fabric puppet with legs. Both puppets will keep babies or small children happy for hours while older children can amuse themselves by creating their own puppet shows.

Peter squeezing under the gate in
The Tale of Peter Rabbit

PETER RABBIT VELOUR
GLOVE PUPPET

Measures: 28 cm (11 in)

YOU WILL NEED

½ m (½ yd) tan velour
23 cm (¼ yd) cream velour
23 cm (¼ yd) blue velour
23 cm (¼ yd) white cotton
1 m (1 yd) blue bias binding
1 square red felt
1 square green felt
dark brown embroidery thread
2 safety eyes
polyester stuffing

From The Tale of Peter Rabbit

TO MAKE

1. Read through the general instructions on pages 12–13.
2. Match the inner arms to the curve on each side of the chest and sew A–B.
3. Place the chest on the back body and sew up both sides.
4. Fold under the bottom raw edge 1 cm (⅜ in), pin and sew.
5. Sew the two ear-liners to the two outer ear pieces, leaving the bottom straight edge open. Turn the right way out. Fold the ears in 5 mm (¼ in) on each side so that they meet in the middle.
6. Pin the ears to the front head, matching the notches and making sure that the ear-liners face the right side of the head. Tack (baste) together and remove the pins. Now, pin the back head to the front head, matching the notches. Sew together and remove the tacking (basting) stitches.
7. Sew closed the chin dart before securing the chin to the side head pieces. Sew closed the side head darts. Pin the side head pieces to the middle head piece,

matching the notches. Sew together, remove the pins and turn right side out.

8. Pierce tiny holes at the eye positions with the end of a small pair of sharp scissors. Insert the eyes through the holes and secure on the reverse with the metal washers provided.

9. Using two strands of embroidery thread, sew a Y stitch (see page 12) for the nose. The bottom stitch should be 13 mm (½ in) long and the two side stitches 10 mm (⅜ in) long.

10. Sew the two pieces of head lining together, leaving the straight edge open. Turn right side out. Slip the lining into the head. Match the side seams of the lining with the darts on the side head and sew the raw edges together, leaving a 5-cm (2-in) opening at the back of the head (see diagram A).

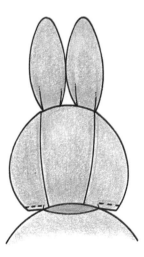

Diagram A

11. Stuff the head through the back opening and then tack (baste) closed.

12. Turn the body inside out. Slide the head upside down into the body until the neck edges meet. Pin the neck edges together, matching the notches, and sew.

Turn the body the right way out and unpick the tacking (basting) stitches.

Jacket

1. Sew closed the dart in the two front jacket pieces. Pin the front pieces to the back piece at the shoulders and sew A–B.

2. Turn under the sleeve edges 5 mm (¼ in) and hem.

3. Sew the front pieces to the back at the sides.

4. Fold the bias binding round the raw outer edges of the jacket, pin and sew. Do the same to the neck edge but leave 15 cm (6 in) of binding at each end to make a tie.

5. Put the jacket on your puppet and tie the neck ribbon in a bow. To stop the jacket coming off, you can sew the bow to the neck seams.

Radish

1. Fold the leaf in half, match the straight edge to the top notch of the radish and pin (see diagram B).

2. Fold the radish in half over the leaf and sew all round the edge between the notches, leaving a gap at the top. Turn the right way out, stuff and sew closed. Tack (baste) the radish to one hand.

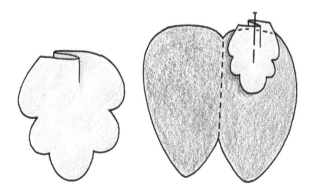

Diagram B

PETER RABBIT FUR FABRIC HAND PUPPET WITH LEGS

Measures: 28 cm (11 in)

YOU WILL NEED

½ m (½ yd) tan fur fabric
23 cm (¼ yd) white fur fabric
small piece white velour
23 cm (¼ yd) blue corduroy
23 cm (¼ yd) blue bias binding
1 square red felt
1 square green felt
brown embroidery thread
2 10-mm (³⁄₈-in) safety eyes
polyester stuffing

TO MAKE

1. Read through the general instructions on pages 12–13.
2. Sew together the two chest pieces, with right sides together, from A to B. Open and lay flat. Pin the inner arms and leg pieces to chest and sew. Remove the pins.
3. Sew the two tail pieces together. Turn the right way out and fold in half. Pin to the back of one of the body pieces between the notches and tack (baste).
4. Match the two body pieces and sew along the back seam C–D. Open and

From The Tale of Benjamin Bunny

remove the tack stitches round the tail.
5. Pin the chest to the body and sew together.
6. Turn right side out. Fold under the bottom raw edge 5 mm (³⁄₈ in), pin and sew.
7. Follow steps 5–12 of the velour glove puppet to complete.

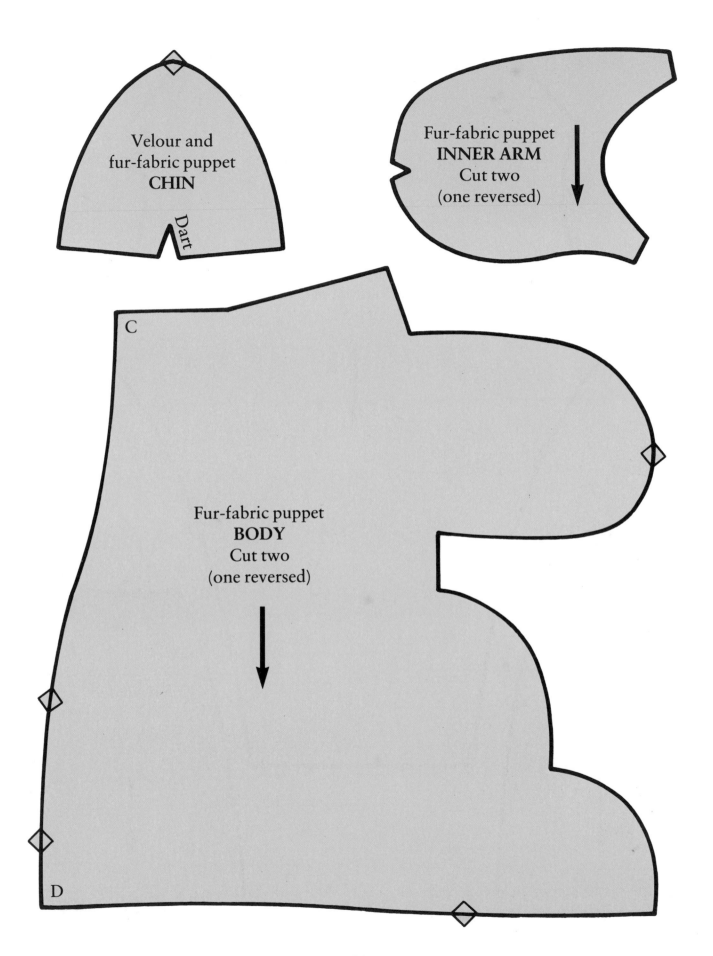

Velour and
fur-fabric puppet
CHIN

Dart

Fur-fabric puppet
INNER ARM
Cut two
(one reversed)

C

Fur-fabric puppet
BODY
Cut two
(one reversed)

D

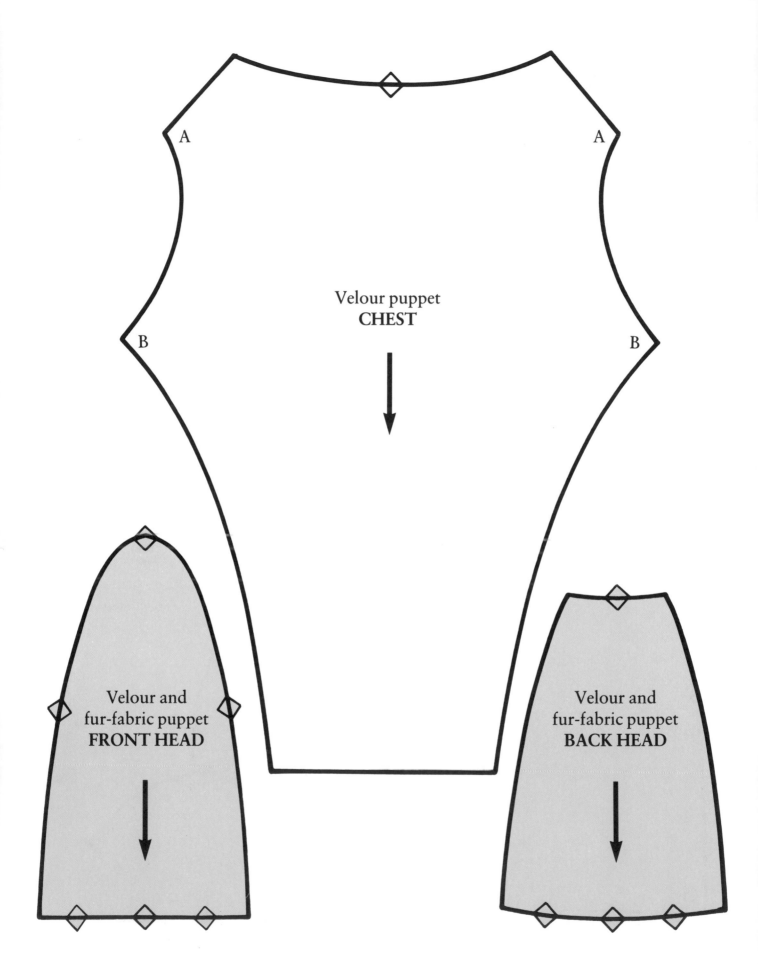

Velour puppet
CHEST

A

A

B

B

Velour and
fur-fabric puppet
FRONT HEAD

Velour and
fur-fabric puppet
BACK HEAD

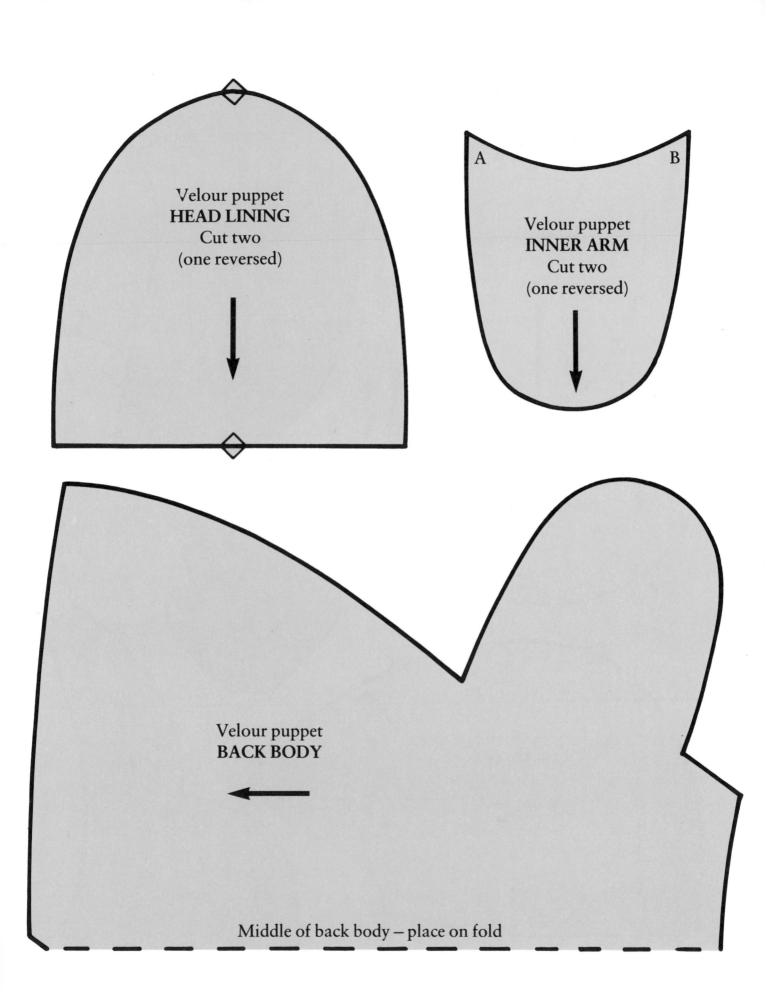

Velour puppet
HEAD LINING
Cut two
(one reversed)

Velour puppet
INNER ARM
Cut two
(one reversed)

A

B

Velour puppet
BACK BODY

Middle of back body – place on fold

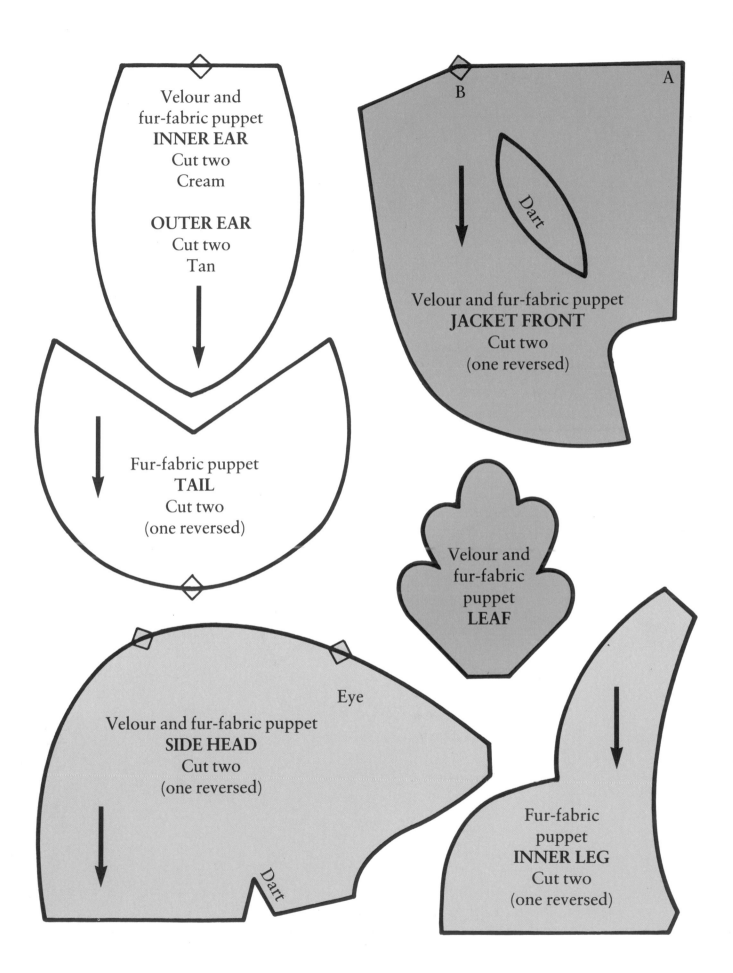

Velour and
fur-fabric puppet
INNER EAR
Cut two
Cream

OUTER EAR
Cut two
Tan

B

A

Dart

Velour and fur-fabric puppet
JACKET FRONT
Cut two
(one reversed)

Fur-fabric puppet
TAIL
Cut two
(one reversed)

Velour and
fur-fabric
puppet
LEAF

Eye

Velour and fur-fabric puppet
SIDE HEAD
Cut two
(one reversed)

Dart

Fur-fabric
puppet
INNER LEG
Cut two
(one reversed)

44

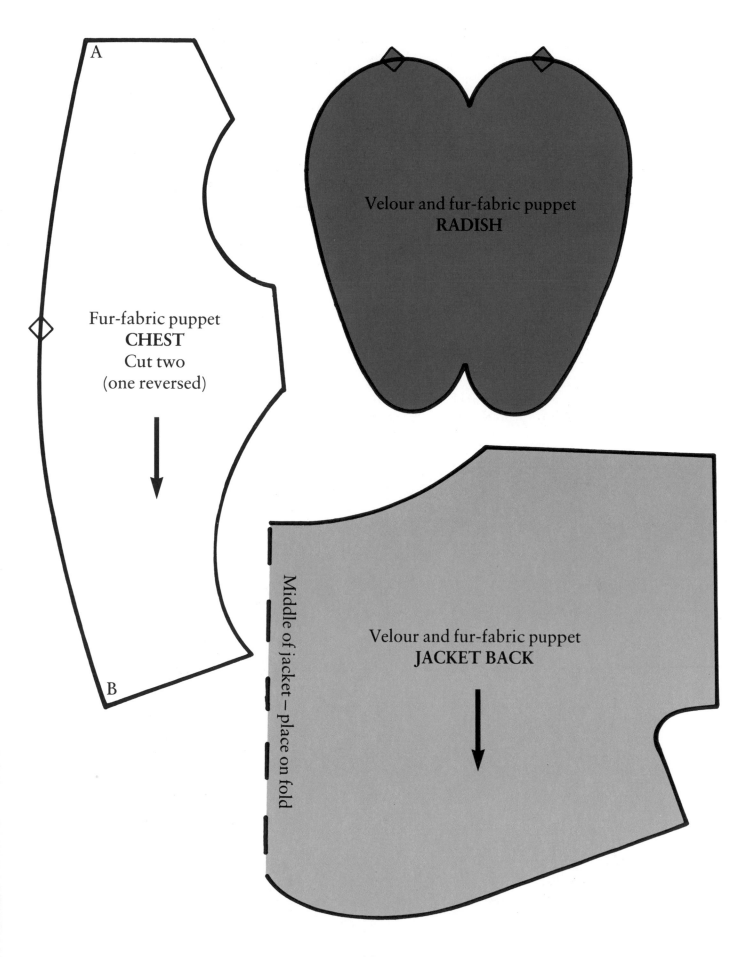

A

Fur-fabric puppet
CHEST
Cut two
(one reversed)

B

Velour and fur-fabric puppet
RADISH

Middle of jacket – place on fold

Velour and fur-fabric puppet
JACKET BACK

45

BEAN BAGS

Measure: 19½ cm (7¾ in)

These delightful character bean bags contain a mixture of polyester stuffing and dried beans so that if they fall over they always stand up again. They are very easy to sew and great fun to play with.

PETER RABBIT
YOU WILL NEED

23 cm (¼ yd) tan velour
small piece of cream velour
23 cm (¼ yd) blue corduroy
1 square red felt
1 square green felt
½ m (½ yd) blue satin ribbon 3 mm
  (⅛ in) wide
2 8-mm (5/16-in) brass buttons
125 g (4 oz/½ cup) dried beans
polyester stuffing
dark brown embroidery thread

TO MAKE

1. Read through the general instructions on pages 12–13.
2. Sew the cream velour ear-liners to the tan velour outer ears, leaving the straight edge open. Turn right side out. Fold the bottom of each ear in on either side so that they meet in the middle.
3. Pin the ears into the large darts on the two side head pieces so that the ear-liners are facing the nose, and sew up the dart.
4. Sew closed the neck dart on both side head pieces.
5. Sew the side heads together, leaving the bottom of the head open, and turn right side out.
6. Pin together the top and bottom pieces for the front and back and sew. Now, sew the front to the back at the shoulders (C–D). Sew the hands to the arms, matching points C and E.
7. To sew the sides together, begin from the bottom notch (F), sew up the side, along the underarms and round the hand.
8. Slide the head upside down into the body until the neck edges meet. Gather the neck to fit the head, pin the head to the neck and sew. Turn right side out.
9. Stuff the head and arms and two-thirds of the body with the polyester stuffing. Do not pack the stuffing in too hard. Fill the remaining space with enough beans to add weight but not so many that it becomes too hard to play with. If the beans are packed in too tightly, the bag is

47

also more likely to split when played with. Hand-sew the bottom and back closed.

10. For the face, take one strand of the embroidery thread and sew a Y stitch for the nose (bottom stitch = 10 mm (⅜ in), side stitches = 7 mm (¼ in)) and French knots for the eyes (see page 13).

To make Peter look rosy, you can apply pink blusher to the cheeks and inner ears.

11. Tie the ribbon round the neck in a bow, trim the ends and sew the middle of the bow to the neck. Sew the two buttons to the front of the body as marked and sew the radish to one hand (to make the radish, see the instructions for the Peter Rabbit velour glove puppet).

HUNCA MUNCA
YOU WILL NEED

23 cm (¼ yd) grey velour
small piece of pink velour
small piece of white cotton
23 cm (¼ yd) pink patterned cotton
black embroidery thread
½ m (½ yd) blue satin ribbon, 3 mm
*   (⅛ in) wide*
125 g (4 oz/½ cup) dried beans
polyester stuffing

TO MAKE

1. Read through the general instructions on pages 12–13.
2. Sew the ear-liners to the outer ears, leaving the straight edge open and turn right side out. Match the notches on each ear to form a pleat and sew across.

3. To complete the head, follow steps 3–5 for Peter Rabbit's bean bag.
4. Make the apron by turning under the outside edge 5 mm (¼ in), then under another 5 mm (¼ in) and sew. Gather the neck edge to 3½ cm (1¾ in) and set aside.
5. Sew the front and back body together at the shoulder seams (A–B). Sew the hands to the arms, matching the points C and A.
6. To sew the sides together, begin from the bottom notch (D), sew up the sides, along the underarms and round the hand.
7. Slide the head upside down into the body until the neck edges meet. Pin at centre back and gather the neck to fit the head. Place the gathered edge of the apron between the edges of the head and the front of the neck, matching the middle notch to the neck, with the right side of the apron facing the head. Tack (baste). Pin the head to the neck all round and sew. Turn right side out.
8. Stuff the head, arms and body, following the instructions in step 9 for the Peter Rabbit bean bag. Hand-sew the bottom and back closed.
9. For the face, take one strand of black embroidery thread and sew a V shape for the nose, so that each side measures 5 mm (¼ in). Use French knots for the eyes (see page 13). Tie the ribbon around the neck in a bow, trim the ends and tack (baste) to the neck.

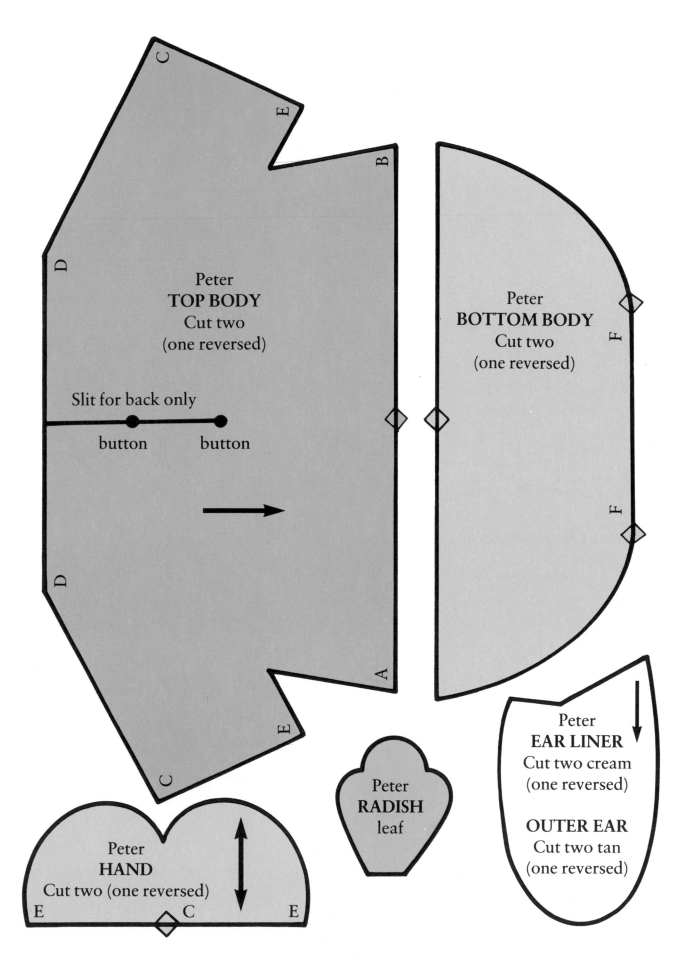

Peter
TOP BODY
Cut two
(one reversed)

Slit for back only

button   button

Peter
BOTTOM BODY
Cut two
(one reversed)

Peter
EAR LINER
Cut two cream
(one reversed)

OUTER EAR
Cut two tan
(one reversed)

Peter
RADISH
leaf

Peter
HAND
Cut two (one reversed)

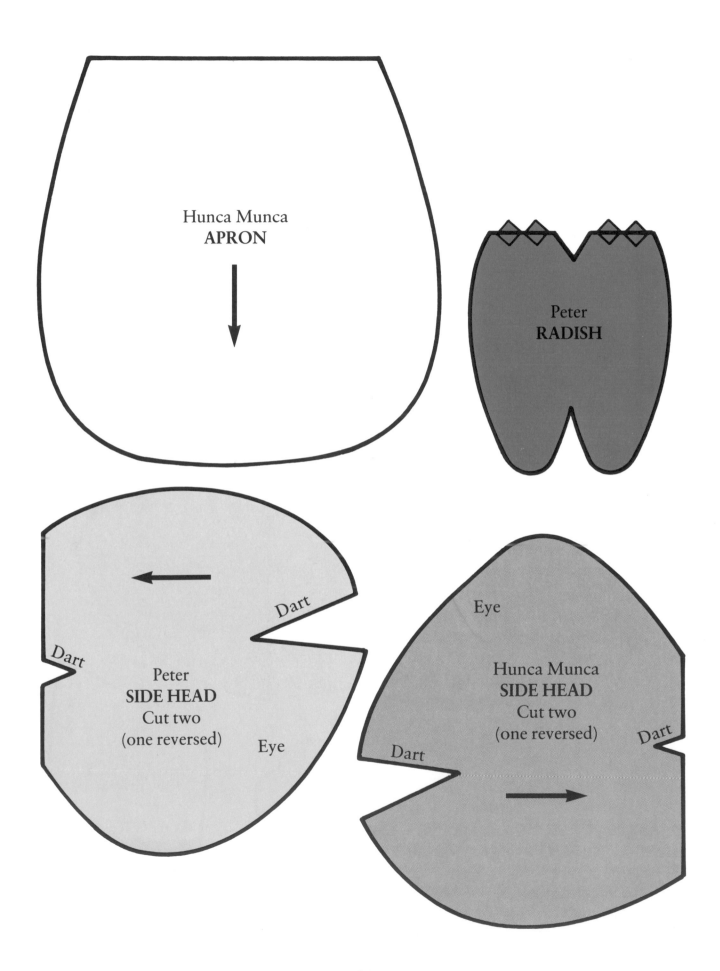

Hunca Munca
APRON

Peter
RADISH

Peter
SIDE HEAD
Cut two
(one reversed)

Dart

Dart

Eye

Eye

Hunca Munca
SIDE HEAD
Cut two
(one reversed)

Dart

Dart

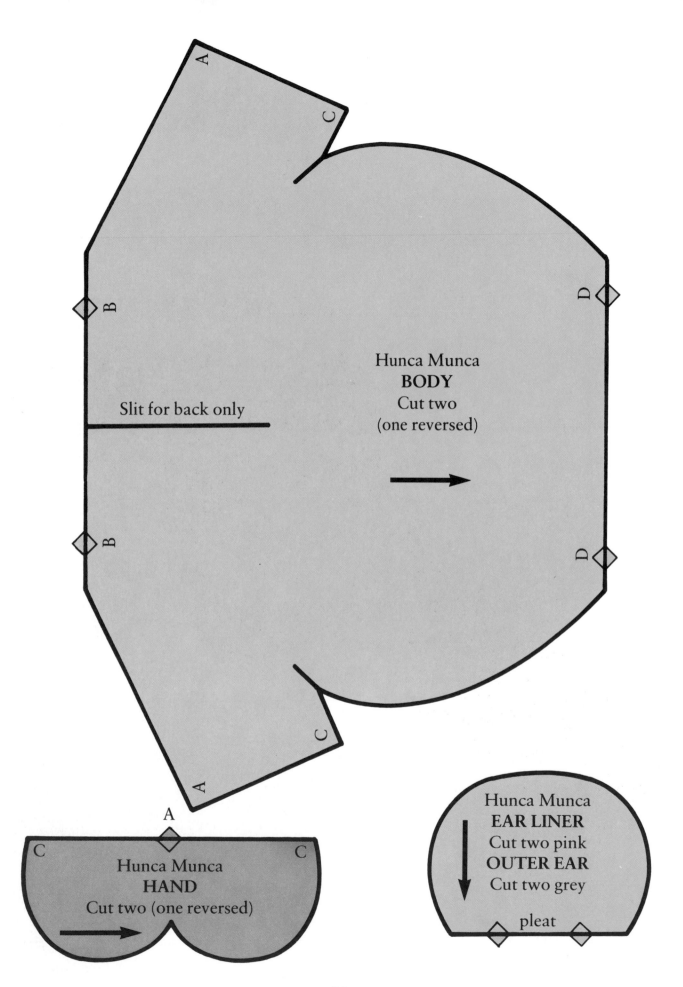

Slit for back only

Hunca Munca
BODY
Cut two
(one reversed)

Hunca Munca
HAND
Cut two (one reversed)

Hunca Munca
EAR LINER
Cut two pink
OUTER EAR
Cut two grey

pleat

A

B

B

C

C

A

A

C

C

D

D

51

SMALL SOFT TOYS
AND FINGER PUPPETS

Measure: approximately 16½ cm (6½ in)

These small soft toys are just the right size for small hands to play with. They are versatile too; the designs here show how you can adapt the toy to make fun finger puppets.

Mouse, Peter Rabbit and Jemima Puddle-duck

PETER RABBIT
YOU WILL NEED

23 cm (¼ yd) tan cotton
23 cm (¼ yd) blue cotton
small piece white cotton
small piece red cotton
23 cm (¼ yd) blue satin ribbon 3 mm (⅛ in) wide
23 cm (¼ yd) green satin ribbon 3 mm (⅛ in) wide
blue, gold and brown embroidery thread
polyester stuffing

TO MAKE

N.B. Press the seams open as you work.

1. Sew the ear-liners to the outer ear pieces, leaving the straight edge open. Turn right side out.
2. Fold the bottom of the ears in at either side so they meet in the middle, and tack (baste).
3. Pin the ears to the slits in the head pieces and sew together.
4. Pin the head pieces together and sew round, leaving the bottom edge open.
5. Pin the collar pieces together and sew round the unnotched edge only. Turn

53

right side out. Pin the collar to the neck of the head, matching the notch to the seam at the back of the head, and sew.

6. Sew the bottom body pieces to the jacket pieces, matching the notches.

7. Pin the sides together and sew, leaving a gap between the notches for stuffing (see diagram A).

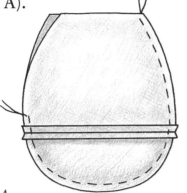

Diagram A

8. Sew the hands to the arms, and then sew the arms together, leaving open the space between the notches for turning. Turn the arms right side out, stuff them and hand-sew the opening closed.

9. Sew the legs together, leaving a gap between the notches. Turn right side out. Stuff the legs and hand-sew the opening closed.

10. Pin the head to the jacket neck and sew round. Turn right side out, stuff and hand-sew the opening closed.

11. Sew the arms and legs to the body, using small tacking (basting) stitches at the points marked.

12. Tack (baste) round the edge of the tail. Place a small amount of stuffing in the middle and then pull the tacking stitches closed. Sew the tail to the back seam, just below the jacket.

13. Sew French knots to make the buttons and eyes (see page 13). Use 3 strands of blue embroidery thread for the eyes and 6 strands of gold for the buttons.

Use 3 strands of brown embroidery thread to sew a Y stitch for the nose (see page 12), and one strand of brown embroidery thread for the whiskers. The whiskers are made by sewing three stitches 6 mm (¼ in) long on each side of the nose.

Tie the blue ribbon in a bow round Peter's neck and sew between the collar at the neck.

Radish

Cut the green ribbon into three 2½-cm (1-in) lengths, and fold each in half. Sew all three together at the bottom and cut the ends. Pin to the radish at the top notch so that the loops are facing downwards (see diagram B). Fold the radish in half and sew round, leaving an opening at one side to stuff (see diagram C). Turn the radish right side out, stuff and hand-sew the opening closed. Tack (baste) to one hand.

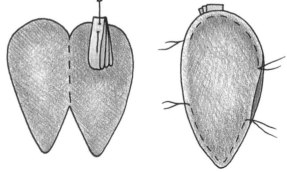

Diagram B   *Diagram C*

Finger puppet

To make the Peter Rabbit finger puppet, follow the instructions for the soft toy until you have completed step 6. Then sew the finger-linings to the bottom body piece between the notches and sew the finger-linings together (see diagram D).

Now continue with the steps for the soft toy, making sure not to sew up the gap for the fingers.

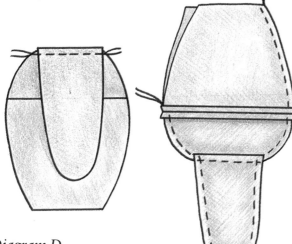

Diagram D

MOUSE
YOU WILL NEED

23 cm (¼ yd) grey cotton
small piece pink cotton
small piece green cotton
dark grey embroidery thread
23 cm (¼ yd) pink satin ribbon 3 mm
*   (⅛ in) wide*

TO MAKE

1. Sew the ear-liners to the outer ear pieces, leaving the straight edge open. Turn right side out.
2. Fold a 5-mm (¼-in) tuck in the middle of each ear and pin into the slits in the head pieces. Sew.
3. Follow steps 4–11 for the Peter Rabbit small toy.
4. To make the tail, use a short length of grey embroidery thread, approx. 6 cm (2½ in) long. Attach it to the back of the body at the bottom by sewing a couple of

The Mouse from The Story of Miss Moppet

small backstitches. Tie a knot at the end of the tail and trim.
5. Embroider the face as for Peter Rabbit, using grey embroidery thread, and tie a pink ribbon round his neck.

Finger puppet
Follow the instructions for the Peter Rabbit finger puppet.

JEMIMA PUDDLE-DUCK
YOU WILL NEED

23 cm (¼ yd) white cotton
small piece blue cotton
small piece yellow cotton
small piece heavy lining
small piece pink print cotton
23 cm (¼ yd) blue satin ribbon 3 mm
*   (⅛ in) wide*
blue and yellow embroidery thread
polyester stuffing

Small children love these little toys

TO MAKE

1. Sew the head of the body together from A to B.

2. Pin the beak to the head, matching the notches and points C and G. Sew to the head and then sew up the beak.

3. Sew the body together from D all the way round to G. Turn right side out, stuff and sew closed.

4. Sew the wings together, leaving the space between the notches open. Turn right side out and sew closed.

5. Sew the feet together, catching the layer of stiffening fabric in between and leaving an opening between the notches. Turn the feet right side out and sew closed.

6. Turn the sides of the shawl in 3 mm (⅛ in) and then another 3 mm (⅛ in), pin and sew.

7. Sew the bonnet sides together. Turn under the raw edge 5 mm (¼ in) and hem. Gather the neck of the bonnet so it measures 5 cm (2 in).

Sew the bonnet brim together along the unnotched edge. Turn right side out and press. Gather the inner edge of the brim between the notches to fit the bonnet. Pin the brim to the bonnet and sew.

Fold the ribbon in half to find the middle and pin it to the back seam of the bonnet. Tack (baste) all round. Sew and remove the tacking (basting) stitches. Leave 8 cm (3½ ins) of ribbon on either side for tying.

8. Sew the wings to the body at the places marked, and then the feet to the bottom of Jemima.

9. Embroider French knots for the eyes (see page 13). Put the bonnet on Jemima's head and tie the ribbon into a bow and sew to the neck. Put the shawl around the neck and tie the ends loosely in a knot.

Finger puppet

Sew the lining pieces to the bottom between notches E and F before following step 1 for the soft toy (see diagram A). To complete, follow the instructions for the soft toy.

Diagram A

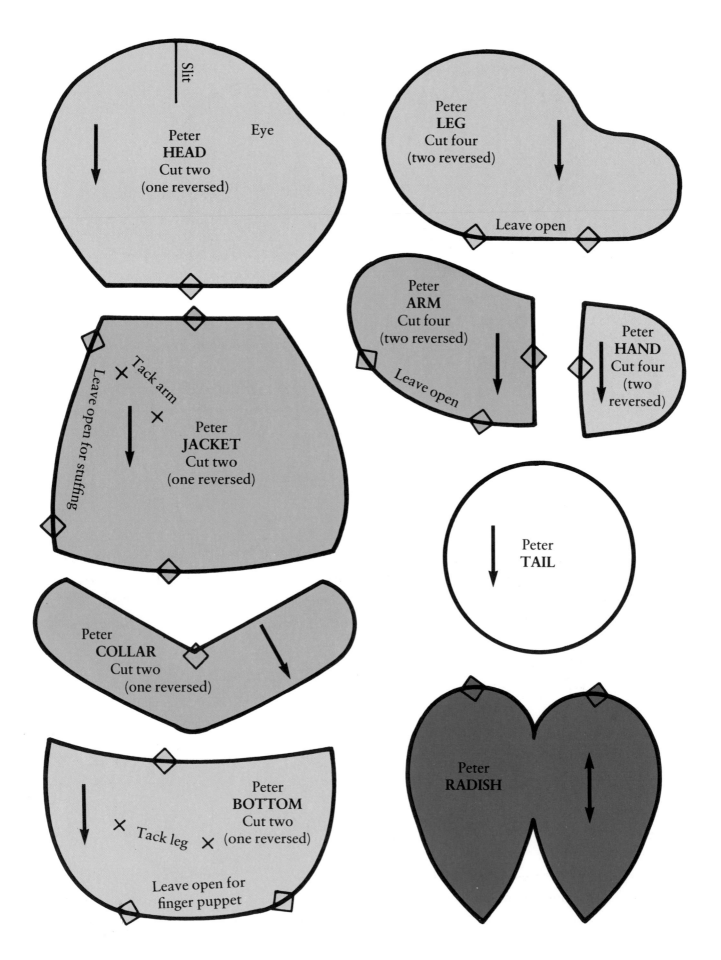

Slit

Peter
HEAD
Cut two
(one reversed)

Eye

Peter
LEG
Cut four
(two reversed)

Leave open

Peter
ARM
Cut four
(two reversed)

Leave open

Peter
HAND
Cut four
(two reversed)

Leave open for stuffing

Tack arm

Peter
JACKET
Cut two
(one reversed)

Peter
TAIL

Peter
COLLAR
Cut two
(one reversed)

Peter
BOTTOM
Cut two
(one reversed)

Tack leg

Leave open for
finger puppet

Peter
RADISH

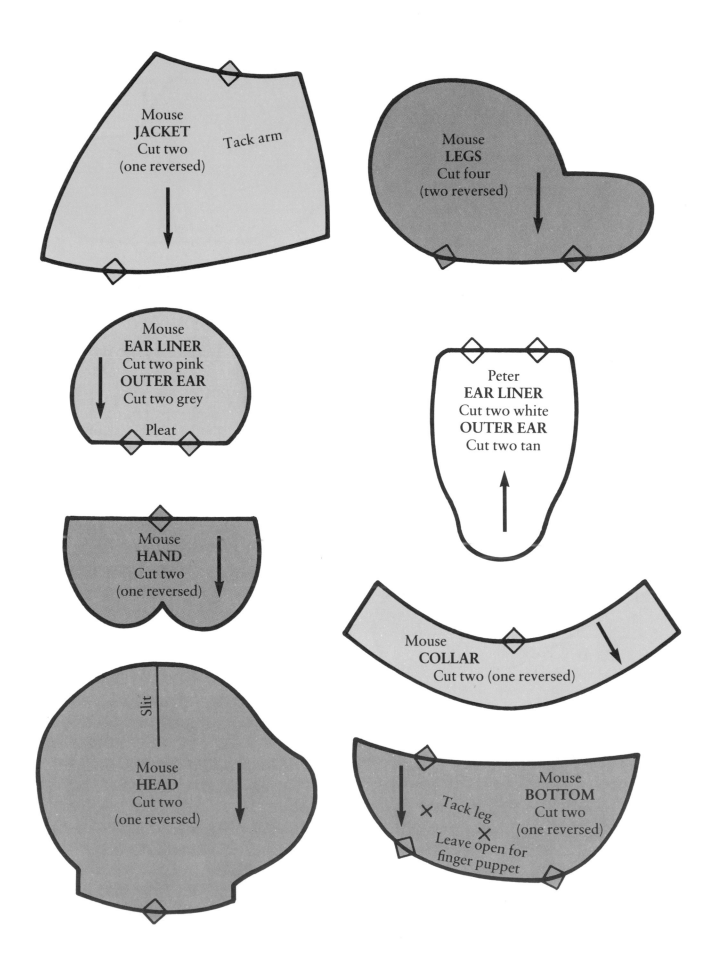

Mouse
JACKET
Cut two
(one reversed)

Tack arm

Mouse
LEGS
Cut four
(two reversed)

Mouse
EAR LINER
Cut two pink
OUTER EAR
Cut two grey

Pleat

Peter
EAR LINER
Cut two white
OUTER EAR
Cut two tan

Mouse
HAND
Cut two
(one reversed)

Mouse
COLLAR

Cut two (one reversed)

Slit

Mouse
HEAD
Cut two
(one reversed)

Mouse
BOTTOM
Cut two
(one reversed)

× Tack leg
×
Leave open for
finger puppet

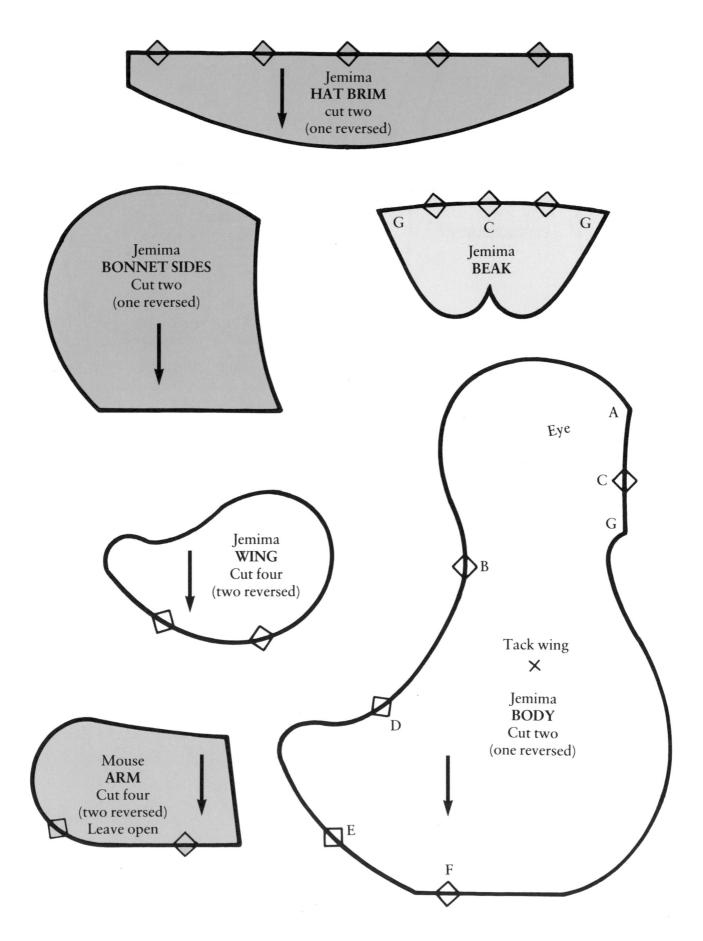

Jemima
HAT BRIM
cut two
(one reversed)

Jemima
BONNET SIDES
Cut two
(one reversed)

Jemima
BEAK

G

C

G

Jemima
WING
Cut four
(two reversed)

Eye

A

C

G

B

Tack wing
×

Jemima
BODY
Cut two
(one reversed)

D

Mouse
ARM
Cut four
(two reversed)
Leave open

E

F

59

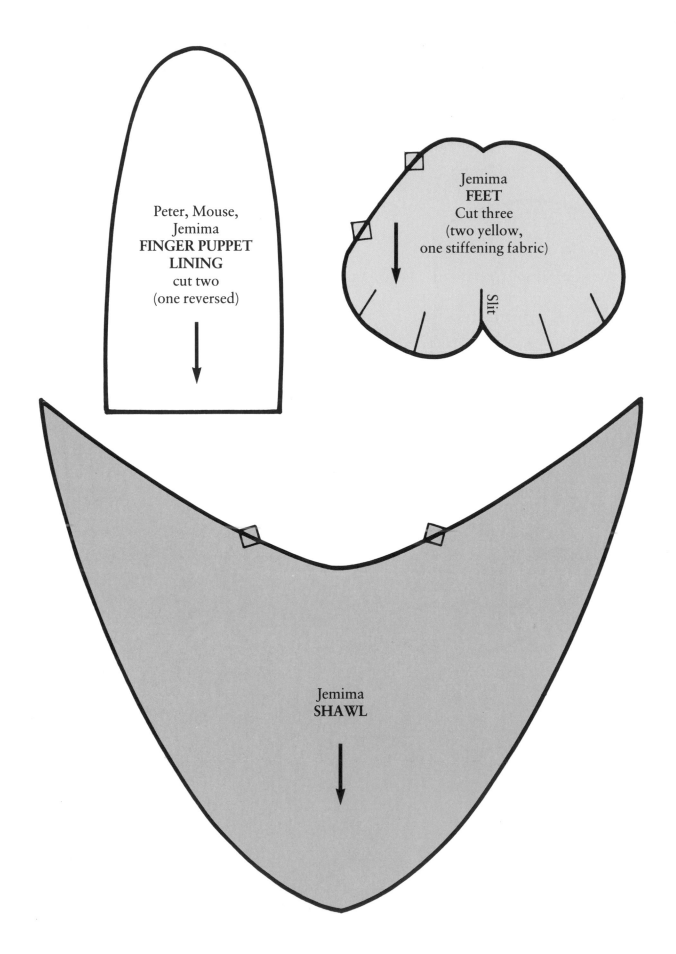

Peter, Mouse, Jemima
FINGER PUPPET LINING
cut two
(one reversed)

Jemima
FEET
Cut three
(two yellow, one stiffening fabric)

Slit

Jemima
SHAWL

PETER RABBIT BALL

This is a delightful toy for a very young child. If you want to vary the design, why not try inserting a bell or chime and sewing a long loop of ribbon so you can hang it from a baby's pram. Alternatively, you could introduce flowers and foliage into the image and add pot-pourri when stuffing the ball to make a pretty pomander.

Two segments of the ball. Painting the background adds life and colour

YOU WILL NEED

½ m (½ yd) white cotton calico
Dylon 'Color Fun' fabric paint in
    jade, pink, red, light blue, dark brown,
    white and yellow
2 sable brushes, fine and medium

1 pencil
water jar and saucers for mixing paint
2 brown waterproof fabric-marking pens,
    fine and superfine
masking tape
polyester stuffing

TO MAKE

1. Tape your fabric on to the pattern with masking tape. Using the pencil, trace the dotted outline, which is the cutting line.
2. Following the general instructions on pages 14–15, trace Peter directly on to your fabric and paint him. When you have finished the first segment, repeat the process three more times so that you have four segments altogether.
3. When the painting is dry, iron the fabric from the wrong side with a very hot iron and then cut out the four pieces carefully.
4. Place two segments right sides together and sew down one curved side. Do the

61

same with the other two segments. You now have the two halves of your ball.

5. Match the seams, right sides together, making sure the images are all the same way up. Pin at the top and bottom. Machine round, leaving a small opening at the bottom.

6. Stuff very gradually, pushing the stuffing in bit by bit until the ball is plump and round. Hand-finish, using tiny stitches to catch the two sides together.

PETER RABBIT BALL PATTERN

POCKET TOYS WITH BAG

Measure: approximately 13 cm (5 in)

Peter Rabbit, Tom Kitten, Jemima Puddle-duck and Mrs Tittlemouse look adorable peeping out of their individual bags. Once you have mastered making the basic toy why not try adapting the designs. You could fill the toys with lavender to make sweet-smelling sachets or you could thread each toy with a loop of lurex thread or cord to make unique Christmas tree decorations.

YOU WILL NEED

For the toys

1 m (1 yd) white cotton calico
Dylon 'Color Fun' fabric paint in jade, pink, red, yellow, light blue, dark brown and white
water jar and saucers for mixing paint
2 sable brushes, fine and medium
pencil
2 brown waterproof fabric-marking pens, fine and superfine
masking tape

From The Tale of Tom Kitten

For the bags

½ m (½ yd) white cotton calico
4 20-cm (8-in) long ribbons, 7 mm (½ in) wide in blue, green, pink and yellow

TO MAKE

1. Following the instructions on pages 14–15, trace and paint each character, taking the paint just beyond the inside pen line. It will really help to look at the illustrations in the original Beatrix Potter books as well as the photographs in this volume when painting the characters.
2. When the paint is dry, iron from the wrong side of the fabric with a very hot iron and then cut out each shape carefully.
3. Match the two halves of the character with right sides together and pin. Sew round on the front side on the inner pen line, leaving the bottom open for stuffing.
4. Clip carefully into all angles as

indicated. Turn, pushing out all the corners and curves, and then iron flat to see if the shape is as you want it.

5. Stuff, using tiny pieces of stuffing at a time, pushing it into the ears with your small blunt tool. Do not stuff too hard – the toys should be only lightly padded.

6. When stuffing Peter Rabbit's ears, pad them only slightly and then machine down the centre to separate them.

7. Hand-finish the bottom edge with tiny stitches.

Bags for the toys

1. Place the fabric over the patterns on pages 70–71 and trace, using a pencil for the border line and the superfine pen for each central character.

2. Paint the designs choosing different colours for the curly border line on each bag.

3. When you have painted, ironed and cut out the square shape, you will need to cut out two more square pieces of calico the same size so that you have three pieces of fabric for each bag.

4. Place the painted square face down on the other two pieces and pin.

5. Sew round the sides and bottom, rounding off the corners.

6. Turn so that the painted piece is on top and iron flat.

7. Hem round the top, sewing the two front pieces together.

8. Attach the ribbon to the front and back of the bag, and pop your toy into the finished bag!

The bags can be adapted too with a bit of imagination. If you attached a much longer ribbon to each side of the bag you could make a little neck purse.

Alternatively, fill the bags with stuffing and sew up the fourth side to make a pin cushion or make a needle case, using the panel as a cover. The designs look pretty, too, as pieces for a simple patchwork pram quilt.

'Mrs. Tittlemouse was a most terribly tidy particular little mouse,' from The Tale of Mrs. Tittlemouse

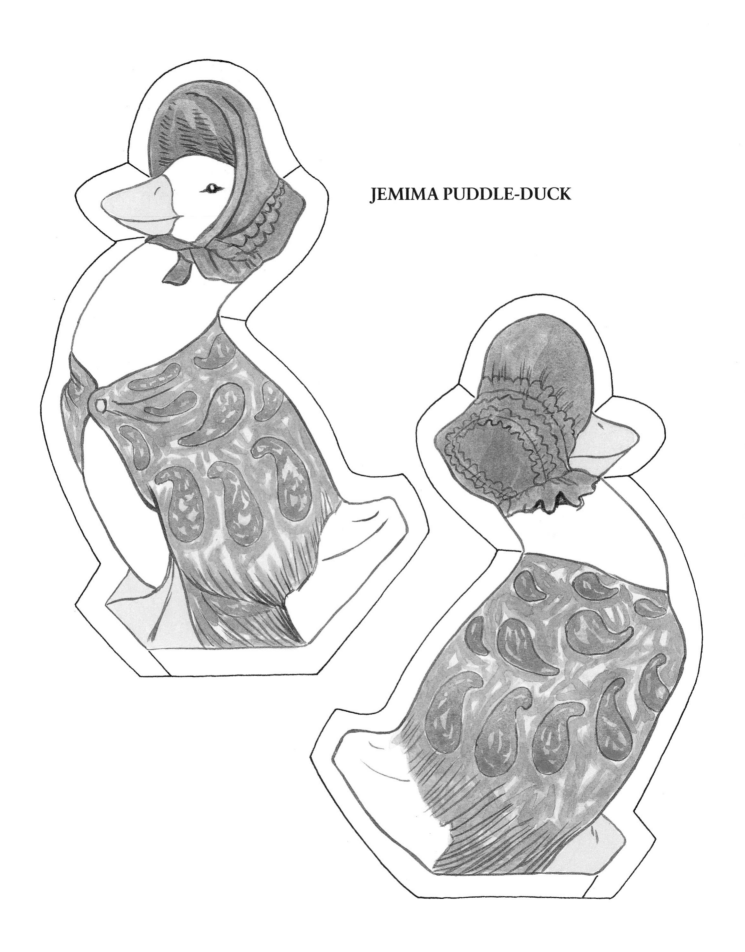

JEMIMA PUDDLE-DUCK

PETER RABBIT

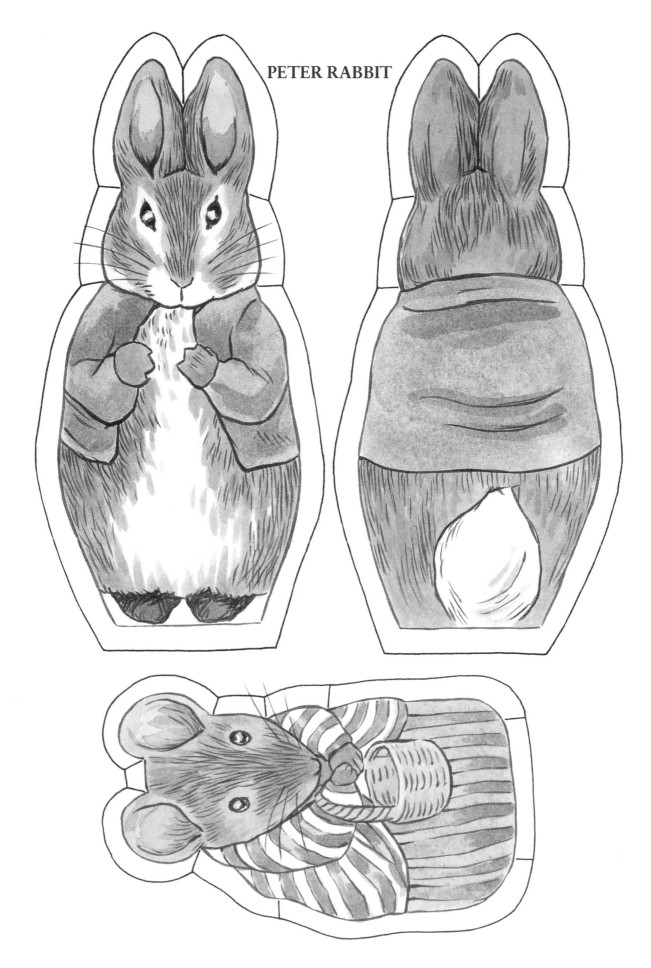

TOM KITTEN

MRS TITTLEMOUSE

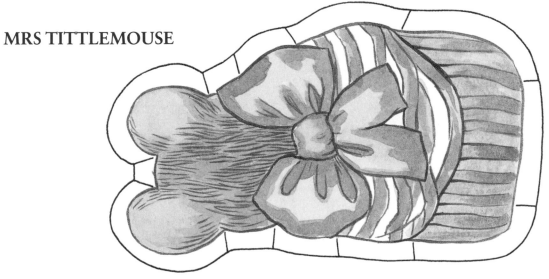

PETER RABBIT BAG

TOM KITTEN BAG

JEMIMA PUDDLE-DUCK BAG

MRS TITTLEMOUSE BAG

POCKET TOY MOBILE

The pocket toys without their bags can be made into this hanging mobile, which makes a very attractive decoration to a room.

YOU WILL NEED

4 pocket toys
wooden embroidery hoop, 15 cm (6 in) in diameter
blue bias binding
fine white cord

TO MAKE

1. Wind the bias binding around the wooden hoop, making sure that none of the wood shows through. When you have completely covered it, stick the ends down with a small blob of glue or secure with a couple of tiny stitches.

2. Cut four pieces of cord, each ½ m (½ yd) long. Fold a length of cord in half to find the middle, tie round the hoop and knot so that you have two equal lengths of cord hanging from the hoop. Do this with the other three lengths of cord equal distances apart.

3. Take the outer piece of the four cords and tie them together at the ends. Trim the ends, leaving one piece of cord longer than the rest to attach to a hook for hanging your mobile.

4. Attach the pocket toys to the hanging cords with a few small stitches at the back of the head.

From The Tale of Mrs. Tittlemouse

PETER RABBIT DRAWSTRING BAG

Measures: 30 × 35 cm (12 × 14 in)

This useful bag is the perfect size for keeping shoes or slippers. You could also make this panel into a cushion or a little shopping bag by adding two cords or fabric handles.

YOU WILL NEED

2 pieces white cotton calico, 30 × 35 cm (12 × 14 in)
paints, brushes and pens as for the soft-toy ball
white silk cord 75 cm (30 in) long.

TO MAKE

1. Trace the Peter Rabbit design on to your fabric and paint, following the general instructions on pages 14–15. Cut out.

2. Place the painted piece of fabric face down on the other piece of calico. Machine round sides and bottom 5 mm (¼ in) from the edge, stopping 5 cm (2 in) from the top at one side. Stitch the hem down 5 mm (¼ in) on each side.
3. Turn the top down 5 mm (¼ in), then another 2½ cm (1 in) so that you have a 2½-cm (1-in) hem to make the channel for the cord, with two outlets to draw it through.
4. Turn the bag right side out and iron. Thread the cord through and knot at the end.

The cover illustration from
The Tale of Peter Rabbit

JEMIMA PUDDLE-DUCK POCKET

Brighten up a child's smock or a dress or apron with this delightful Jemima pocket.

YOU WILL NEED

*white cotton calico 14 × 14 cm
(5½ × 5½ in)*
*paints, brushes and pens as for the soft-
toy ball*

TO MAKE

1. Trace and paint the Jemima Puddle-duck design on to your fabric following the instructions on pages 14–15, and cut out.
2. Turn down a narrow double hem at the top of the pocket and sew.
3. Place the pocket upside down and right side down on garment (see diagram). Pin, and machine along bottom edge 5 mm (¼ in), leaving 5 mm (¼ in) each side.
4. Turn back the pocket, turn the sides in, iron and hem.

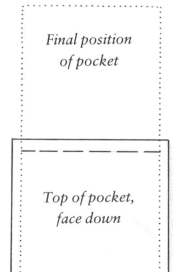

Final position of pocket

Top of pocket, face down

JEMIMA PUDDLE-DUCK POCKET PATTERN

PETER RABBIT DRAWSTRING BAG PATTERN

BENJAMIN, on the contrary, was perfectly at home, and ate a lettuce leaf. He said that he was in the habit of coming to the garden with his father to get lettuces for their Sunday dinner.

(The name of little Benjamin's papa was old Mr. Benjamin Bunny.)

The lettuces certainly were very fine.

1866

KNITTING AND NEEDLEPOINT

Knitting and needlepoint are wonderful skills to acquire; they do not require expensive equipment and the materials are usually small enough to be portable so you can work on your designs wherever you are.

Beatrix Potter's paintings of animals and flowers translate beautifully into designs for knitting and needlepoint and even rug-making. Peter Rabbit and Squirrel Nutkin are reproduced in fine detail in cross-stitch to make babies' bibs, Jemima Puddle-duck's ducklings adorn a knitted pram cover, Hunca Munca decorates a nursery sampler and Mrs Tittlemouse falls asleep by the fire on a luxurious tufted hearth rug.

HUNCA MUNCA SAMPLER

This sampler depicts Hunca Munca from The Tale of Two Bad Mice *tidily sweeping with her dustpan and brush. Beatrix Potter's dates are embroidered at the top and the names of the two dolls whose house Hunca Munca and Tom Thumb break into are embroidered at the bottom.*

Hunca Munca, from The Tale of Two Bad Mice

HUNCA MUNCA SAMPLER

Measurements: approximate size of finished embroidery 25 × 28 cm (10 × 11¼ in)

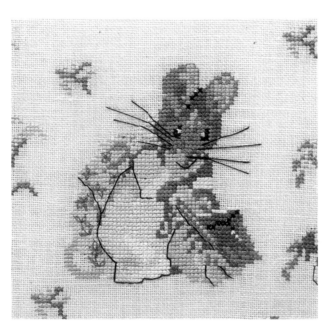

Detail of the sampler

YOU WILL NEED

round embroidery frame
masking tape
*Coats Anchor Stranded Cotton: 1 skein
   each of colours 1, 49, 105, 128, 131,
   145, 206, 257, 259, 260, 288, 339,
   355, 368, 376, 403, 872, 886, 889,
   888, 969 and 979*
*32-count Charles Craft Classic Reserve
   100% linen fabric 38 × 46 cm
   (15 × 18 in)*

tapestry needle, size 24 or 26
*picture frame with white backing board
   to fit*
N.B. You can work the sampler on
a larger or finer mesh fabric but, of
course, you will need to adjust the
amount of stranded cotton required
accordingly.

TO MAKE

1. Before you begin stitching, prepare
your fabric by oversewing the raw edges
or binding them with masking tape to
prevent fraying.
2. To make accurate working easier, find
the centre point of the fabric: run a line of
tacking stitches widthways and
lengthways, to correspond with the
arrows on the chart on pages 84–87.
Where the lines meet is the centre point.
3. Stretch the fabric in a large round
embroidery frame until the material is
quite taut and easy to work on.
4. By counting the squares on the chart,
find the centre square and start your
needlepoint on the corresponding point
on your piece of fabric. The chart will tell
you which colour cotton to use.

5. Take 2 strands of cotton and work your cross-stitch over 2 strands of fabric, making sure that the top stitches of the crosses all lie in the same direction (see page 86). Work outwards from the centre until you have finished Hunca Munca and then move on to the outer pattern, following the chart and counting the squares.

6. Now, with 1 strand of colours 105 and 257, embroider a few lazy daisy flowers and leaves on Hunca Munca's dress.

7. Embroider all whiskers, bees' legs and antennae in backstitch as indicated with 1 strand of colour 403. Then, still using 1 strand of colour 403, use backstitch to outline Hunca Munca's nose, lower edges of sleeve, apron, edge of overskirt, brush handle and bristles, Squirrel Nutkin's toes and the base of Peter Rabbit's tail.

8. Press your work carefully on the wrong side with a warm iron and a damp cloth.

9. Mount your embroidery on a white backing board as shown in Figs 1–3. Place the embroidery centrally over the backing board, fold surplus canvas to the back and secure at the top with pins into the edge of the board. Pull firmly over the lower edge and pin in position. Repeat for

Unfinished drawing of foxgloves, possibly a study for The Tale of Jemima Puddle-duck, *1908*

the side edges, pulling the canvas until it lies taut over the board, Secure at the back by lacing across both ways with stout thread; remove pins and place in frame.

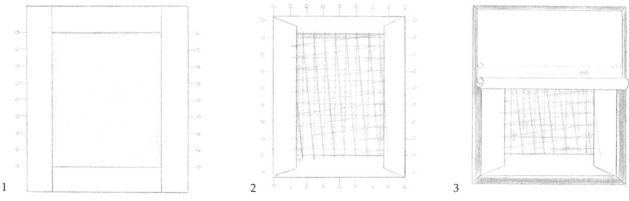

Figures 1, 2 and 3: *mounting canvas on a backing board, lacing across it wrong side to secure*

CHART

*Top half of Hunca
Munca sampler*

KEY

1	·
49	
105	
128	☒
131	
145	
206	◤
257	
259	
260	❘
288	
339	⊙
355	
368	
376	✚
403	
872	◢
886	
888	·
889	
969	
979	

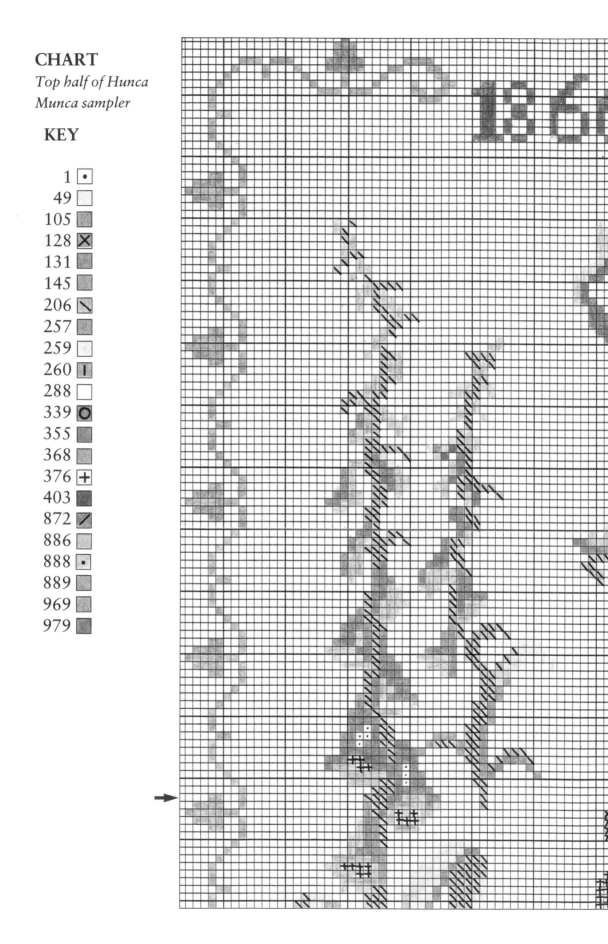

84

CHART

Bottom half of Hunca Munca sampler

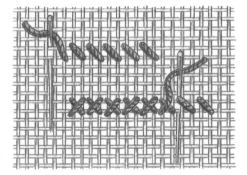

Cross-stitch

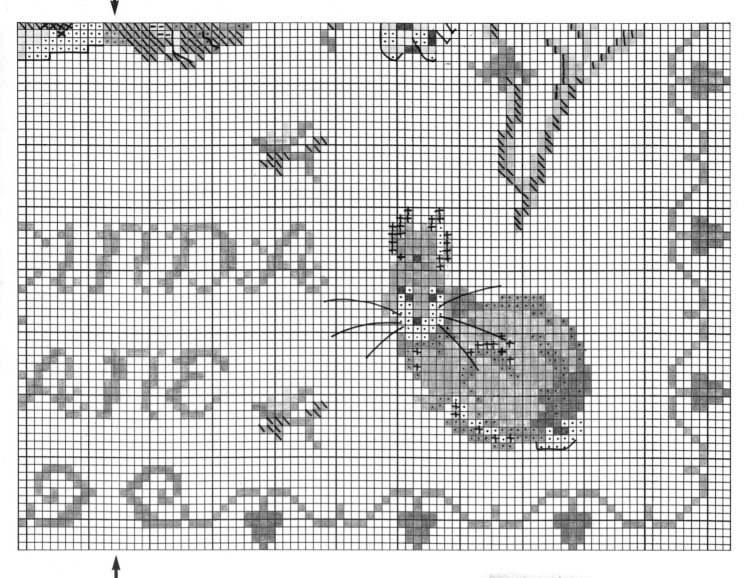

'Once upon a time there were four little Rabbits, and their names were . . .' From The Tale of Peter Rabbit

TUFTED RUG AND KNITTED SHAWL

The charming design used for this rug of Mrs Tittlemouse asleep by the fire, combines with the attractive shape to make it ideal for laying in front of a fireplace; the glowing colours will be warming too.
The triangular knitted shawl will also keep you warm as well as looking pretty with its tasselled borders and lacy effect. Knitted with a thick silky wool, it makes a really luxurious garment which is soft enough to wrap a baby in.

'She was too tired to do any more.'

MRS TITTLEMOUSE
SEMI-CIRCULAR TUFTED RUG

Measurements: 127 × 70 cm (50 × 27½ in)

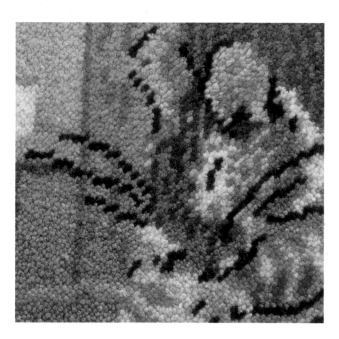

Detail of the rug

YOU WILL NEED

*Nottingham Group Turkey Action packs
(160 pieces per pack)
1 each of colours 205, 838, 877, 901,
943; 2 each of colours 863, 929, 978;
3 each of colours 932, 941; 4 of colour
501; 6 of colour 939; 8 of colour 900;
9 of colour 973; 11 of colour 203;
13 of colour 983; 18 of colour 930.
(N.B. For stockists of the above, write,*

*enclosing a self-addressed envelope, to
Atlascraft Ltd, Ludlow Hill Road,
West Bridgeford, Nottingham
NG2 6HD)
3⅓ mesh interlock rug canvas 142 × 91
cm (56 × 36 in)
latchet hook
3 m (3 yd) of carpet braid for binding
edges
strong sewing thread*

TO MAKE

1. Rug-making is most simple if you sit at
a table with one end of the canvas facing
you, so that the knots are worked on the
line of canvas that lies on the edge of the
table; a weight placed on the unworked
canvas will assist in supporting the
worked part of the rug.
2. The knots can be made by following
either Method 1 or Method 2 shown
below. They are equally quick and the
only difference is that the pile lies in
different directions. This can be turned to
advantage to enable two people to work
at the rug from opposite ends of the

canvas towards the middle. If one person uses Method 1 and the other Method 2, the complete pile will lie in the same direction.

3. One selvedge will be upper edge of the rug chart. Always work in rows across the width of the canvas from selvedge to selvedge. Knot through every stitch following the chart on pages 92–93. Do not work blocks of colour separately.

4. To finish the edges of the rug, first cut away the excess canvas on curved edges approximately 5 cm (2 in) from the edge of the rug. Pin back the excess canvas, including selvedge. Pin the carpet braid in position round the outer edge and stitch down. Stitch down the inner edge, making darts as necessary on curves to keep the braid flat.

5. To give the rug a smooth, even surface, clip any long ends with sharp scissors; this will give the rug a professional finish, but care must be taken. Remove loose ends with sticky tape or a damp cloth.

Mrs. Tittlemouse cleaning up after Mr Jackson, from The Tale of Mrs. Tittlemouse

Rug care and cleaning

Shake out loose dirt and vacuum clean both sides of the rug. Lightly clean the pile with a cloth or brush moistened in liquid detergent. Light hand-shampooing machines may be used. Dry by hanging the rug on a line away from direct sunlight. The rug may be cleaned professionally.

Do not attach any backing material, such as hessian. Do not use a washing machine or allow the rug to become soaking wet. Do not use heavy, electrical or commercial shampooing machines. Do not tumble dry.

'Your very good health, Mrs. Tittlemouse!'

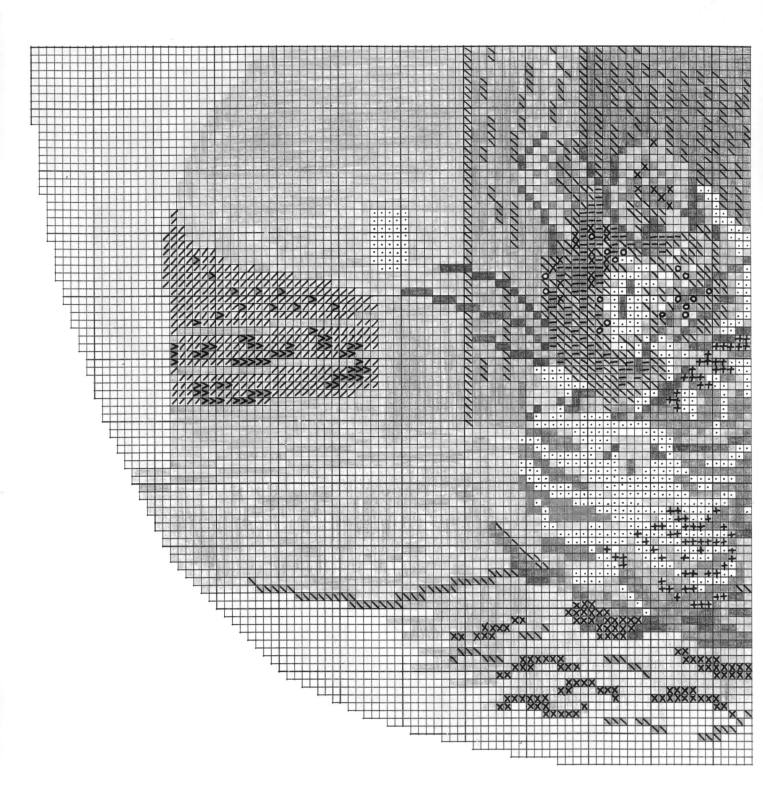

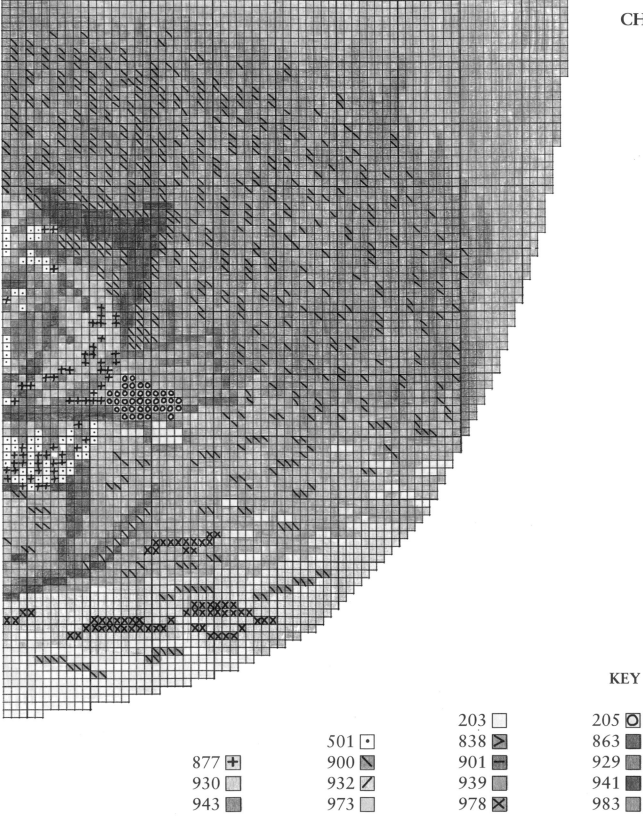

CHART

KEY

		203 ☐	205 ◎
	501 ⊡	838 ▶	863 ▨
877 ✚	900 ◩	901 ⊟	929 ▨
930 ▨	932 ◪	939 ▨	941 ▨
943 ▨	973 ▨	978 ⊠	983 ▨

93

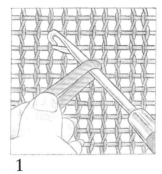 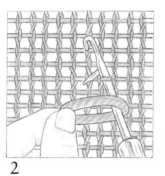 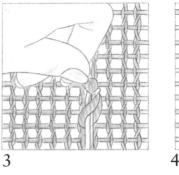 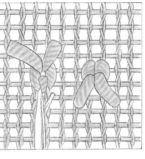

1   2   3   4

RUG-KNOTTING, METHOD 1

1. Fold one piece of wool exactly in half round the shank of the hook; the evenness of the pile depends on this precise fold.
2. Push the hook under the strands of canvas (weft) where the knot is to be made.

3. Ensure the latch is free to open, place the free ends of the wool through the hook and turn it slightly to the right.
4. Pull the hook through the loop of wool and push hook forward. Gently pull the two ends of the wool to make the knot firm.

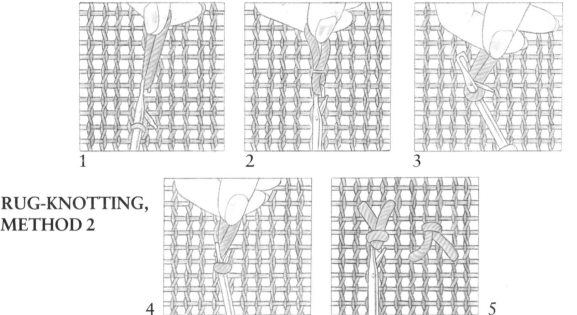

1   2   3

RUG-KNOTTING, METHOD 2

4   5

1. Push the hook under the strand of canvas (weft) where the knot is to be made until the latch lies behind the canvas. Fold one piece of wool in half and place this in the hook, ensuring the two ends are exactly the same length.
2. Pull the hook back towards you so that about a third of the wool is in front and two thirds behind the canvas weft threads.

3. Ensure the latch is free and open and place the free ends of the wool through the hook. Then allow the latch to close over the wool.
4. Place the free ends of the wool through the hook and let the latch close.
5. Pull the hook backwards through the loop of wool and gently pull the knot to make it firm.

KNITTED TRIANGULAR SHAWL

Measurements: approximate depth at point, excluding fringe, 76 cm (30 in)

Under side of shawl fringe showing knots

YOU WILL NEED

9 balls (50 g) Patons or Astra Waverley
Gold DK in cream
pair of 5 mm/No 6 needles
row counter
crochet hook

Tension

20 sts and 26 rows to 10 cm (4 in) over stocking stitch.

Abbreviations

K = knit; P = purl; Kb = K into back of st; Pb = P into back of next st; sts = stitches; patt = pattern; Lp1 = make loop by wrapping yarn round right needle; yfwd = yarn forward; tog = together; sl = slip; psso = pass slipped st over; C7F = slip next 4 sts on cable needle to front of work, Kb, P2, now Kb, P2, Kb across sts on cable needle; C7B = slip next 3 sts on cable needle to back of work, Kb, P2, Kb, now P2, Kb across sts on cable needle; MPK = pick up horizontal strand lying before next st and place on left needle, then P1, K1 into it; MKP = pick up horizontal strand lying before next st and place on left needle, then K1, P1 into it; rep = repeat; cm = centimetres; in = inches.

TO MAKE

Centre section
Cast on 3 sts.
1st row: Lp1, K3.
2nd row: Lp1, K1, P1, K2.
3rd row: Lp1, K to end.
4th row: Lp1, K1, P to last 2 sts, K2.

95

5th and 6th rows: As 3rd and 4th. (9 sts)
7th row: Lp1, K2, K2tog, yfwd, K1, yfwd, sl 1, K1, psso, K2.
8th row: As 4th.
9th row: Lp1, K2, K2tog, yfwd, K to last 4 sts, yfwd, sl 1, K1, psso, K2.
10th row: As 4th.
11th and 12th rows: As 9th and 10th. (15 sts)
13th row: Lp1, K2, (K2tog, yfwd, K1) twice, (yfwd, sl 1, K1, psso, K1) twice, K1.
14th row: As 4th.
15th row: Lp1, K2, (K2tog, yfwd, K1) twice, K to last 7 sts, (yfwd, sl 1, K1, psso, K1) twice, K1.
16th row: As 4th.
17th and 18th rows: As 15th and 16th. (21 sts)
19th row: Lp1, K2, (K2tog, yfwd, K1)

3 times, (yfwd, sl 1, K1, psso, K1) 3 times, K1.
20th row: As 4th.
21st row: Lp1, K2, (K2tog, yfwd, K1) 3 times, K to last 10 sts, (yfwd, sl 1, K1, psso, K1) 3 times, K1.
Continue in this way widening lace 'V's and introducing a new 'V' on 4th row following, then on every following 6th row until shawl measures 61 cm (24 in), ending after a wrong-side row.
Next 11 rows: Lp1, K to end.
Cast off loosely.

Borders (2)
** Cast on 161 sts using the two needle method and knit 1 row (do not knit into back of sts).
Work in cable rib pattern thus:
1st row: K1, Kb, P1, Kb, MPK, *P3, Kb, (P2, Kb) twice; rep from * to last 7 sts, P3, MKP, Kb, P1, Kb, K1.
2nd row: (K1, Pb) 3 times, *K3, Pb, (K2, Pb) twice; rep from * to last 9 sts, K3, (Pb, K1) 3 times.
3rd row: K1, Kb, (P1, Kb) twice, MPK, *P3, Kb, (P2, Kb) twice; rep from * to last 9 sts, MKP, (Kb, P1) twice, Kb, K1.
4th row: (K1, Pb) 4 times, *K3, Pb, (K2, Pb) twice; rep from * to last 11 sts K3, (Pb, K1) 4 times.
5th row: K1, Kb, (P1, Kb) 3 times, MPK, *P3, Kb, (P2, Kb) twice; rep from * to last 11 sts, P3, MKP, (Kb, P1) 3 times, Kb, K1.
6th row: (K1, Pb) 5 times, *K3, Pb, (K2, Pb) twice; rep from * to last 13 sts, K3, (Pb, K1) 5 times.
7th row: K1, Kb, (P1, Kb) 4 times, MPK, *P3, Kb, (P2, Kb) twice; rep from * to last 13 sts, P3, MKP, (Kb, P1) 4 times, Kb, K1.
8th row: (K1, Pb) 6 times, *K3, Pb, (K2,

Fleecy Flock's wool shop from The Tale of Little Pig Robinson

Pb) twice; rep from * to last 15 sts K3, (Pb, K1) 6 times.

9th row: K1, Kb, (P1, Kb) 5 times, MPK, *P3, Kb, (P2, Kb) twice; rep from * to last 15 sts, P3, MKP, (Kb, P1) 5 times, Kb, K1.

10th row: (K1, Pb) 7 times, *K3, Pb, (K2, Pb) twice; rep from * to last 17 sts, K3, (Pb, K1) 7 times.

11th row: K1, Kb, (P1, Kb) 6 times, MPK, *P3, C7F; rep from * to last 17 sts, p3, MKP, (Kb, P1) 6 times, Kb, K1.

12th row: (K1, Pb) 8 times, *K3, Pb, (K2, Pb) twice; rep from * to last 19 sts, K3, (Pb, K1) 8 times. (185 sts)

On these 12 rows one repeat of the cable pattern has been worked with 2 increasings inside edge ribbing at both ends of rows on every right-side row. Work 16 more rows. (217 sts)

Next row: Rib 32, MPK, *P1, drop next st off needle, P1, K2tog, P1, Kb, P1, K2tog; rep from * to last 35 sts, P1, drop 1, P1, MKP, rib to end. (175 sts)**

Next row (on which holes for tassels are worked): K1, (yfwd, K2tog, K1) to end. Knit 1 row. Cast off.

Now run down dropped stitches to cast-on edge.

Make another piece the same but working C7B in places of C7F.

TO MAKE UP

1. Block borders by pinning out round edges, wrong side facing, then press lightly with a cool iron and a dry cloth.
2. Join side edges of centre section to cast-on edges of borders. Now join centre seam at lower edge.
3. Cut remaining yarn into 30-cm (12-in) lengths. Taking 4 strands for every tassel and use crochet hook to make a knot in every hole along cast-off edge of border.
4. Press seams, then press tassels and trim evenly.

'That little old woman was surely a mouse,' from Appley Dapply's Nursery Rhymes

JEMIMA PUDDLE-DUCK
PRAM COVER

Measurements: approximately 61 × 91 cm (24 × 36 in)

You do not have to be an expert fair-isle knitter to make this lovely pram cover with Jemima's ducklings, but you do need a little patience initially. The satisfaction of producing a piece of picture knitting is immense and makes the effort well worth while.

Detail of the duckling motif

YOU WILL NEED

7 balls (50 g) Patons Beehive Soft Blend
   Chunky in blue
1 ball each (50 g) Patons Beehive Soft
   Blend Chunky in white and gold
pair 6 mm/No 4 needles

length of black embroidery thread

Tension
15 sts and 20 rows to 10 cm (4 in) over stocking st.

Abbreviations
K = knit; P = purl; sts = stitches; g st = garter st; inc = increase, increasing; tog = together; beg = beginning; rep = repeat; B = Blue; G = Gold; W = White.

TO MAKE

With B, cast on 80 sts. Work 8 rows in g st.
Next row: K6, P1, (inc purlways in next st, P7)8 times, inc in next st, P2, K6. (89 sts).
Next row (right side): K.
Next row: K6, P77, K6.
Rep the last 2 rows until work measures 24 cm (9½ in) from beg, ending after a

CHART

Read odd rows K from right to left and even rows P from left to right.

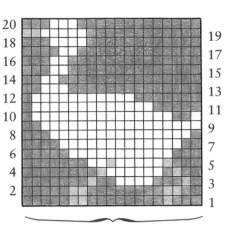

20 18 16 14 12 10 8 6 4 2

19 17 15 13 11 9 7 5 3 1

19 pattern sts

Use a separate small ball of G for each G area and a separate ball of B on row 3 to 12 at each side of the duck's body. Twist yarns on wrong side when changing colour.

wrong-side row.
Work Puddle-ducks from chart thus:
1st row: K, 21B, work 1st row of chart, 49B.
2nd row: K6B, P43B, work 2nd row of chart, P15B, K6B.
3rd to 20th rows: Rep 1st and 2nd rows 9 times but working rows 3 to 20 of chart.
21st to 26th rows: Work 6 rows all in B as before.
27th row: K, 35B, work 1st row of chart, 35B.
28th row: K6B, P29B, work 2nd row of chart, P29B, K6B.
29th to 46th rows: Rep 27th and 28th rows 9 times but working rows 3 to 20 of chart.
47th to 52nd rows: Work 6 rows all in B as before.
53rd row: K, 49B, work 1st row of chart, 21B.
54th row: K6B, P15B, work 2nd row of chart, P43B, K6B.
55th to 72nd rows: Rep 53rd and 54th rows 9 times, but working rows 3 to 20 of chart.

Continue in B only as before until work measures 76 cm (30 in) from beg, ending after a K row.
Next row: K6, P1, (P2 tog, P7)8 times, P2 tog, P2, K6. (80 sts).
Change to g st and work straight until piece measures 91 cm (36 in), ending after a wrong-side row. Cast off *loosely*.
Press on the wrong side with a cool iron and a dry cloth. Embroider an eye in black on each Puddle-duck.

Hints for motif knitting

It is worth the time to take a pair of needles and oddments of yarn and knit a trial piece from the chart you are going to knit, allowing about four extra stitches at each side of the motif in the background colour. This will give you an idea of how many small balls of yarn in each colour you need to cut off ready before you start. By winding off a small ball (sometimes only a few centimetres/inches) of yarn for each colour area, you will avoid a criss-cross effect at the back of the work, which might make the fabric bulky and distorted.

Do not be tempted to use larger balls of yarn than required, as they drag on the work and can be difficult to disentangle. Do not knot new colours, but leave the end hanging on the wrong side; it can then be gently tightened afterwards to the correct tension and neatly darned in on the wrong side, taking care not to distort the right side of the fabric.

CROSS-STITCH BABIES' BIBS

Measurements: length at centre front 20 cm (8 in)

Peter Rabbit and Squirrel Nutkin feature on these delightful babies' bibs in pink and blue. Once you have made the bibs you could use the motif designs to embroider all sorts of items, like a cushion cover or a pillowcase.

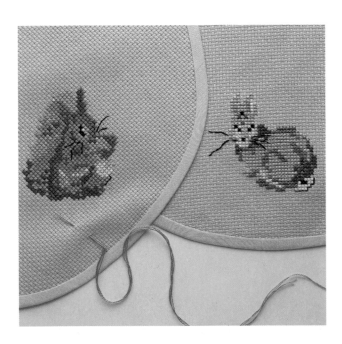

Detail of Squirrel Nutkin and Peter Rabbit in the cross-stitch design

YOU WILL NEED

Coats Anchor stranded cotton

For Squirrel Nutkin

1 skein (or a few lengths) each of colours 1, 260, 339, 355, 368, 376, 403, 886, 888 and 889.

For Peter Rabbit

1 skein (or a few lengths) each of 1, 355, 376, 403, 886, 888, 889 and 969.

For each bib

14-mesh embroidery fabric 30 × 25 cm (12 × 10 in)
size 24 tapestry needle
bias binding
sewing thread
1 button

TO MAKE

1. Make the bib pattern following the instructions on the reduced pattern on page 103. Fold the embroidery fabric in half on the grain, pin the pattern to it and cut out.
2. Bind the neck edge of the bib with bias binding and then bind the outer edge.
3. Sew a button to one back neck edge, then work a loop with some strands of embroidery thread to correspond on the other edge.

101

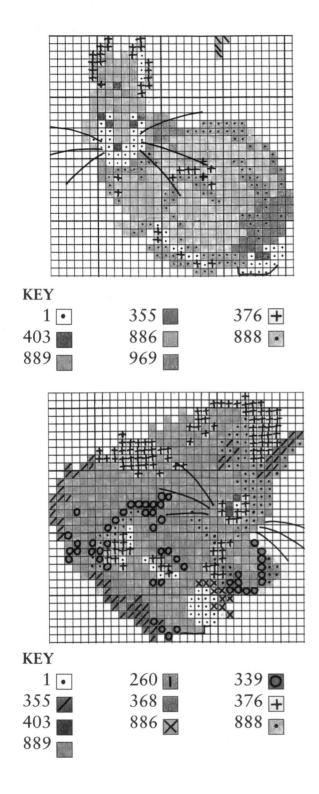

KEY

1 ⊡	355 ■	376 ⊞
403 ■	886 ■	888 ⊡
889 ■	969 ■	

KEY

1 ⊡	260 ▥	339 ◉
355 ◪	368 ■	376 ⊞
403 ■	886 ⊠	888 ⊡
889 ■		

Each square on the chart represents one cross-section of threads.

5. Begin at the centre and ensure that the top stitches of crosses all lie in the same direction.

6. Now with 1 strand of colour 403 embroider the whiskers, Squirrel Nutkin's toes and Peter Rabbit's tail using backstitch.

7. Press work on the wrong side using a warm iron and a damp cloth.

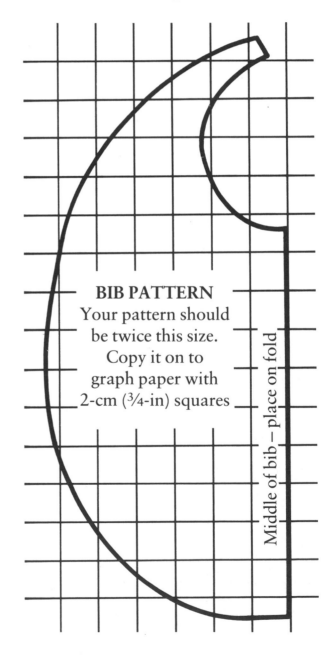

BIB PATTERN
Your pattern should be twice this size.
Copy it on to graph paper with 2-cm (¾-in) squares

Middle of bib – place on fold

4. The bib is now ready to embroider. Using 2 strands of cotton, embroider the squirrel or rabbit motif, following the charts above and work in cross-stitch over one strand of fabric (see page 86).

DECORATING FURNITURE

What could be better than a nursery full of
furniture designed specially for your colour scheme
and your child. Decorated wooden furniture can be
horrendously expensive to buy, but a few pots of
paint or some paper cut-outs, together with some
patience and a little time, can turn ill-matching
odds and ends into a really lovely nursery set. It's
wonderfully satisfying to come back from a junk
shop, a jumble sale or a foray into the loft with
some dilapidated remnants and then stand back, a
few evenings later, in front of a chest or a chair you
can hardly recognize. And a piece you have
decorated yourself, perhaps with a new baby's
name and birthdate, makes a personal gift that is
bound to be doubly appreciated.

GENERAL INSTRUCTIONS

Original Peter Rabbit stencil designs from the 1920s

STENCILLING

Materials

Base paints   The ideal base paints to use are ordinary emulsions, which can be protected after stencilling by a couple of coats of acrylic or polyurethane varnish. Vinyl silk emulsion gives a harder, smoother finish than matt emulsion, but you may find the stencil paint doesn't take so readily to this surface, and you'll need to paint over the design a couple of times. Oil-based eggshell paints will provide a tougher finish still.

If you can't find quite the colour you want, mix a couple of shades together, or lighten one with white paint (of the same type, of course, and in small amounts to begin with). The little colour-test pots of paint are invaluable for smallish items of furniture: one or two will probably be enough for the base coat, especially if you mix them with white paint or a small amount of water. But do try to make sure you have some of the base paint left over, in case you need to touch up any mistakes on your stencilling. It's also a good idea to paint a couple of sheets of paper with the base paint so that you can try out your stencil and see how it looks against the background colour.

If you want to stencil straight on to gloss paint that is in good condition, simply sand it down lightly so that the paint has a surface to which it can grip.

Stencil paints   Acrylic paints, sold in tubes, are probably the best ones to use when stencilling furniture; they're widely available in a range of colours and dry quickly. (This is a point to remember when blending shades or diluting them to

106

the right consistency: don't mix so much paint that it dries before you can apply it.) You can also use emulsion-type hobby paints and varnish over them for protection, or use spray paints. Because they are much quicker than brush paints to apply, spray paints are ideal when you have a large area to stencil (a border right round a room, for example), but are not quite so suitable for the more detailed designs in this book which require small amounts of specific colours in specific places. The paint is not as easy to control, so the area around the stencil itself must be fixed down firmly with masking tape so that paint doesn't drift underneath. Wear a mask and open all the windows, and keep children and pets away.

Stencil brushes Proper stencil brushes are well worth buying. They are available in a variety of sizes; you'll need at least a couple of the smallest size, about 4 mm (1/8 in) across, for the detailed designs in this book (three or four would be ideal – then you won't have to wash them out so often). The short stubby bristles are designed to dab paint straight down on to a surface so that it doesn't seep under the stencil holes. The longer, softer bristles of an artist's brush give a flowing stroke, but stencil painting is more a matter of stippling on the paint, a little at a time, to build up the required intensity of colour and produce a lightly textured finish. If you get too much paint on the brush it will flood under the stencil, blurring the outlines of the design.

Stencil card Stencils can be cut from a variety of materials, but stencil card is the best. It is treated with linseed oil so that it resists paint, and is fairly easy to cut. If

you cannot get this card in an art or craft shop, you could use acetate, which has the advantage of being transparent, but it is a lot more difficult to work with.

Varnish Acrylic varnish is probably the easiest to use. Keep your brush moistened with water and dilute the varnish with water if necessary. It is not quite as hard-wearing as polyurethane varnish, however, which is a better choice if the item of furniture is going to get a lot of hard use.

Preparing the furniture
You may find it takes as much time preparing your item of furniture as it does actually stencilling on the design, but careful preparation really does pay off. New wood should have any rough edges sanded down, followed by a coat each of

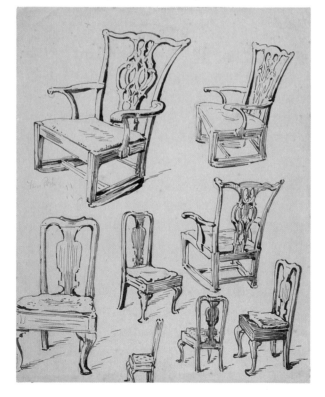

Studies of 'Chippendale' and Queen Anne chairs, 1903

primer and undercoat, before the base paint is applied. Lightly rubbing down the surface with fine sandpaper between each coat produces a smoother finish and helps each layer of paint to meld with the next. Old wood should be checked for woodworm, and uneven or peeling paint should be sanded down or removed completely, using one of the readily available paint strippers. Any holes and cracks can then be filled with an all-purpose filler, which should be sanded down when dry. A layer of undercoat, and you'll be ready to apply the base paint on to which the design will be stencilled.

Cutting the stencil

Trace the design you want to use on to tracing paper with a pencil, remembering to rule a line along the base of the pattern to help you position the stencil straight. Rule a line on the stencil card and position your tracing in place along it. Fix the tracing paper to the card with masking tape, slip a piece of carbon paper under the tracing paper and draw over the image again.

Fix your stencil sheet to the cutting surface with masking tape, which won't tear or mark it. You can buy special cutting boards, which have a particularly smooth surface that doesn't scar; otherwise a vinyl tile, a piece of plywood or an unmarked chopping board will do. Carefully cut out the design with a craft knife, trying not to leave any rough or jagged edges. If you should cut through any of the stencil 'bridges', don't panic – simply mend the cut by covering it with a patch of strong sticky tape on both sides,

trimming off the excess with the craft knife.

FOR DÉCOUPAGE

Materials

Eggshell paint, or matt or vinyl emulsion, will provide the best background for varnishing over; gloss paint has too much of a surface shine and won't take varnish. A nice idea is to choose a background colour you like, in a fairly definite shade (small test pots of paint are ideal here and go a surprisingly long way), then mix some of it with white paint of the same type for your base coat, keeping a little of the original paint for a decorative border or flourishes around the pictures.

Cutting out the pictures

Try to guide the paper through the scissor blades rather than pushing the scissors through the paper, and cut from underneath the paper to keep your hand out of the way and allow a good view of what you're cutting. Small inner sections can be cut away by first making a small hole in the waste area with the point of your scissor blade, then cutting out the rest from underneath. Cut out these interior pieces first, then the rest of the picture.

You can just about cut out mice tails, if you are careful. Leave a paper border around the tail until you are ready to stick it down, then trim this away at the last minute, to avoid accidental damage. Whiskers are extremely difficult! It's probably better to add them on later with a fine brush and some black paint.

STENCILLING

Stencilling is an ideal way of making furniture more individual and introducing a nursery theme. Mistakes are quite easy to put right and, if the worst comes to the worst, you can simply paint over the whole design and try something else. Toy boxes, cribs, cots, chests of drawers, cupboards and mirror frames look delightful stencilled, and you can use borders or individual motifs to accentuate any unusual features the piece might have.

Detail of Jemima Puddle-duck stencil design

YOU WILL NEED

stencil card
craft knife
masking tape
tracing paper
base paints

stencil paints
stencil brushes
fine paintbrush
absorbent kitchen paper

TO APPLY

1. Trace the designs on to the stencil card and cut out, following the general instructions on pages 107–108.
2. Make a few practice prints from the stencil before starting on your piece of furniture. If you've painted a couple of sheets of paper in your background colour(s) as advised in the general instructions, you'll be able to see how the finished design looks against it and gain confidence in your technique at the same time.
3. Estimate how your pattern will fall. If you are stencilling a border round a toy box, for example, work out whether you're going to be able simply to apply

109

STENCILLED TOY TRUNK

An old tin trunk can easily be transformed into a fun toy box with a few coats of paint (over red oxide metal primer) and some carefully applied stencils.

The trunk photographed here has been painted in pale blue eggshell to provide a tough finish and complementary background for the Puddle-duck stencils. The darker blue inside the trunk perfectly sets off the smaller yellow ducklings.

The cover illustration for The Tale of Jemima Puddle-Duck

The Mouse from The Story of Miss Moppet *makes a very good stencil design*

the stencil twice, say, and neatly fill one side, or whether you'll have to repeat a smaller device from the stencil (such as the ducklings in the Jemima Puddle-duck design). You'll probably be able to do this visually by laying down the stencil sheet and making a few small pencil marks. To be extra safe, make a paper pattern of the area, pencilling on the design to give yourself exact measurements. It's sometimes helpful to stencil from the left- and right-hand edges towards the middle, leaving a smaller space in the centre, which is then easier to fill in accurately.

If you are going to position the motif in a less structured way – say, in the centre of a box lid, or rotating round a central image – a paper pattern is invaluable for working out spacing and showing you how the design will look.

4. Draw a pencil line along the surface you are going to stencil so that your border or motif will be straight, lay the stencil sheet in position with its base line on the pencil line and fix it on with masking tape.

5. Assemble your stencil brushes, a fine paintbrush for touching up mistakes, your stencil paints and a little of the base coat, a damp cloth for wiping away any splashes, and some absorbent kitchen paper for blotting excess paint from your brush. Acrylic paints can be squeezed on to a saucer or palette and thinned with water, if necessary. The paint should be the consistency of thick custard: if it's too thin, it will flood under the stencil.

6. Load your brush with paint, dab it on the kitchen paper a few times so that it is not too heavily charged, and begin to fill in the stencil outlines, working from the edge of the shape towards the centre.

7. Fill in every area of the colour you are working with, changing or washing the brushes for each fresh colour. When you have completed every section, wait a few seconds for the paint to dry (or at least to be dry enough not to run when you lift up the card), and then carefully take off your stencil.

8. If you find some edges are smudged, don't despair! You can carry out miraculous repairs with a fine brush, using stencil paint if the damage is not too severe, or base coat if you have departed radically from the outline you were aiming for. Wipe over the stencil sheet

Peter Rabbit looks very effective stencilled on this lampshade and chair. The radish adds a bit of colour.

with a damp cloth from time to time to avoid paint building up and smudging the outlines.

9. When the design is quite dry, apply a couple of coats of varnish, sanding lightly between each one. A soft brush gives the smoothest finish when varnishing. Keep this brush for varnishing only; old paint on a brush can seep into the varnish and give a very muddy look, quite spoiling the effect after all that trouble. Or you can spray on polyurethane varnish from a can. Varnishing brings the colours right up, particularly if you have been using emulsion paints for the base and the design.

Jemima Puddle-duck with her ducklings

THE PETER RABBIT DESIGNS

There are two types of stencil design given on pages 116–117. The first, featuring Peter Rabbit with a radish and Jemima Puddle-duck with a duckling, is more detailed and suitable for wider borders – along a toy chest, for example, or a chest of drawers. You will need blue, brown, green, red and white paints for a Peter Rabbit border, and blue, pink, white and yellow for Jemima Puddle-duck. You can add more space between the figures to fit the given area, or repeat the smaller motifs to fill an awkward gap.

The second type of design is much simpler and therefore quicker to apply, though you'll have to be careful to dab paint in every corner of the figures, as

The smaller and simpler stencil designs only require one colour. White works well against a coloured background.

they are quite small and detailed. The rabbits, ducks and mice can race along the back of a chair or top of a crib or cot, in whatever colour you like. Hold down the small bridges of stencil card with your thumbnail to make sure all the details come out.

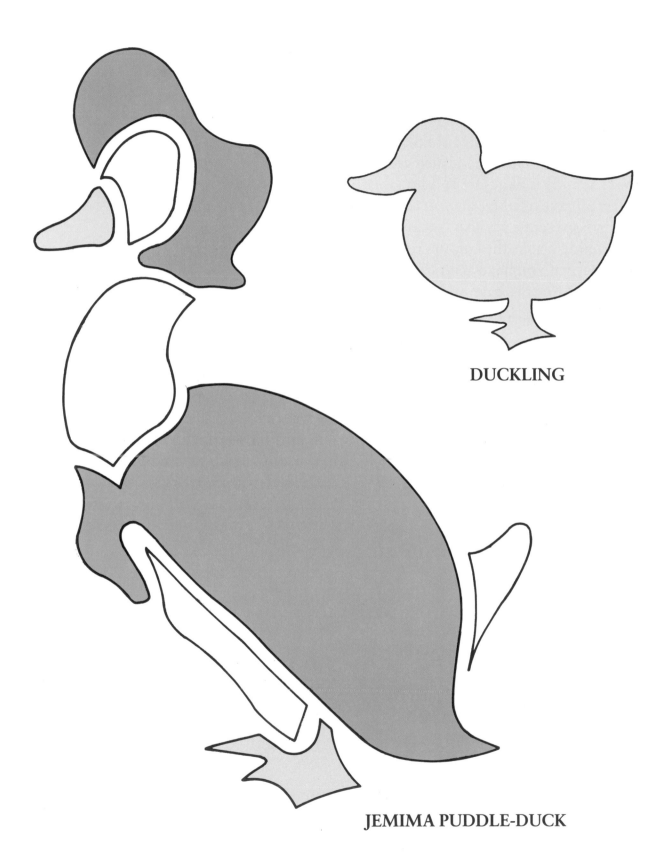

DUCKLING

JEMIMA PUDDLE-DUCK

116

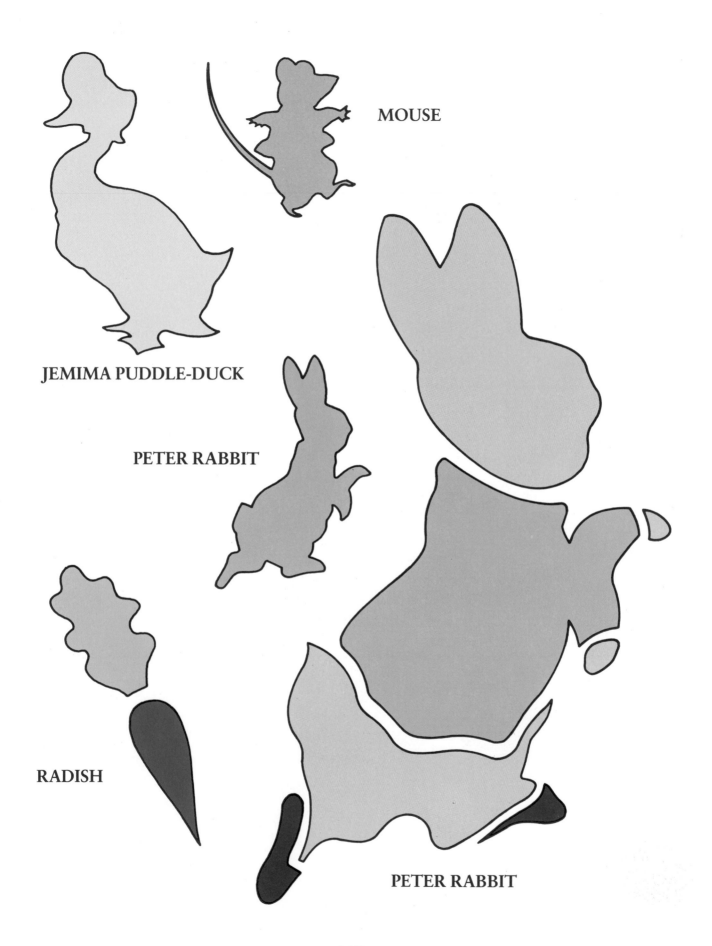

MOUSE

JEMIMA PUDDLE-DUCK

PETER RABBIT

RADISH

PETER RABBIT

DÉCOUPAGE

Découpage – the colouring, cutting out, assembling and gluing of paper motifs on to screens, fans, boxes, tables, chairs and many other items of furniture – is a craft that was particularly popular in the eighteenth century.
You can create delightful pieces by grouping the Peter Rabbit pictures together in an attractive design against a sympathetic background, perhaps unifying the design with a simple hand-painted border. A few coats of varnish will give a durable finish and help the pictures cohere with the painted background.

Close-up detail of découpage coat hanger and hook

YOU WILL NEED

small pair of scissors, with sharp,
*   preferably curved, blades*

eggshell base paint
blu-tack (display adhesive)
glue
varnish and brush

From The Tale of Mr. Jeremy Fisher

119

From The Tale of Squirrel Nutkin

TO MAKE

1. Prepare your surface for decorating, as described in the stencilling section on page 108 and paint your background colour.

2. You will find Beatrix Potter pictures to be cut out on pages 130–135. You can, of course, cut pictures from copies of the Peter Rabbit books if you would prefer a wider selection or have specific favourites in mind, but do buy a replacement copy if you are cutting up a cherished story!

3. Group the pictures on your chosen item of furniture. Small blobs of blu-tack (display adhesive) are useful for holding them in provisional place while you stand back and take a critical look. (Blu-tack/ display adhesive may leave a mark on an emulsioned surface, but this should disappear when the piece is varnished.) Swapping or moving pictures is simplicity itself, so you can try endless variations until you're quite happy with the result.

4. When you're satisfied with the arrangement of pictures, lightly mark their position in pencil and take them off, a few at a time, for gluing. Spray adhesive is very neat and will allow you to reposition the pictures if necessary, or you can use wallpaper paste. Smooth out any air bubbles with your finger.

5. To bring the pictures together, you might want to add a border, as in the box shown in the photograph. It's probably easier to draw a pencil line with a ruler, so that you can be sure the border will be straight, and use it as the basis for a simpler painted design. Practise on a spare piece of paper, with a fine brush, until you can produce confident, fluent strokes.

6. Paint the varnish on when any paint is quite dry with a soft brush, which you should keep for varnishing only so that there's no chance of any old paint seeping in to spoil the job. Use quick, short strokes, all in the same direction, and be on the look-out for drips or runs, taking them off with the brush or your finger. You will need about eight coats, and each of them should be light and even, to build up a smooth finish. Let each coat of varnish dry for at least six hours.

PETER RABBIT AND FRIENDS
WOODEN CUT-OUTS

These large plaques, cut from plywood and painted with acrylics, look lovely grouped along a nursery wall and will delight small children. The shapes are easily transportable, and can be hung in a different bedroom if your child has to give up the nursery to a new baby.

YOU WILL NEED

tracing paper
carbon paper
masking tape
4 mm (⅛ in) plywood – if you are going to make all 4 plaques you'll need 4 pieces at least 35 × 30 cm (14 × 12 in). It's sometimes sold in sheets 610 × 915 mm (2 × 3 ft) so one would be enough, cut into 4 equal sections (the shop should do this for you).
fretsaw, plus some spare blades
sandpaper
primer
medium-sized paintbrush
white spirit
emulsion paint
acrylic paints: blue, brown, white and black for Peter; brown, dark green, red, yellow, white and black for Benjamin; blue, pink, yellow, white and black for Jemima; pink, green, brown, white and black for Mrs Tiggy-winkle

2 paintbrushes – fine and extra fine
acrylic varnish and soft brush
stick-on tab and ring to hang up the figure

TO MAKE

1. Trace the outlines on pages 125–128 including all the details.
2. Draw a rectangle in pencil round each tracing, then divide the rectangle into equal, numbered squares. Draw a second

From The Tale of Benjamin Bunny

121

rectangle twice the size of the first on another piece of paper, and divide it into the same number of squares as the first one. Number these squares and copy whatever is in the original, smaller square on the larger one. You should end up with a fairly accurate double-size duplicate.

3. Tape your first shape to a piece of plywood and slip under it 2 sheets of carbon paper, taped together to be large enough. Draw around the outer line only, which will be your cutting line, then remove the paper and carbon. (Keep the tracing safe; you'll need it later.)

4. Find a work surface at a comfortable height for you to saw. Holding the shape down firmly with one hand so that the cutting line sticks out from the edge of the table, draw the fretsaw down once or twice and start to cut. Cut from underneath the piece of wood, on a downward stroke – make sure the blade and handle are facing in the direction you want the saw to go. When you have cut as far down the length of the wood as the U-shape of the saw will allow, carefully draw the blade out again and start from the other end.

If the plywood splinters a bit at the edges, don't worry – sanding down will take away most of the roughness, and you can fill in any larger cracks with all-purpose filler, sanding again when it has dried.

5. Smooth round the edges of the piece with sandpaper, then apply a coat of primer to one side. Prime the other side when the first is dry. Apply 2 coats of emulsion to each side. These will act as an undercoat for the acrylic paint and provide a coloured border for your

shapes, so you may want to choose a colour that tones with the nursery paint or wallpaper.

6. When the shape is quite dry, lay your tracing over it, matching up the cut edges, and tape the tracing to the plywood figure. Slip the carbon paper underneath and transfer the details.

7. For painting the figures, refer to the Peter Rabbit books, if you have them, to see the colours Beatrix Potter used, as well as looking at the photographs here and reading the more detailed advice on each figure given below.

Acrylic paints are easy to blend with each other. Highlighting and shading fur or clothes looks very effective; add a little white or black to the main colour to mix subtle shades. If you don't like the effect, you can always just wipe it off with a damp cloth or paint over it. Add definition by outlining each part in darker paint with a fine brush; don't use a felt-tip pen, which will run when you varnish the figure.

8. Apply a couple of coats of acrylic varnish with a soft, wide brush, to protect your plaque and keep the colours glistening freshly.

9. Stick on the hanging ring. You may have to experiment a little to find the right position for the plaque to hang straight; Jemima's ring, for example, needs to be on her body rather than her head or she will tilt to one side.

Peter Rabbit

See the pattern for the shading of Peter's fur: paler around the eyes, tummy and lower part of the body; darker on the rest of the face and beneath the coat. The blue coat can be quite flat; if you like add details of the sleeve and collar later with a fine brush.

Benjamin Bunny

The red pom-pon and spotted handkerchief (used for carrying onions) look lovely and bright, and are easy to paint. Mix a spot of black with the red for shading and outlining. His fur is paler along his tummy, the sides of his face and the inner ear, darker towards the tail; you can outline the fur with a speckled dark brown line.

Jemima Puddle-duck

Jemima's crowning glory is her bonnet; it looks extremely effective if you highlight the rim and the top in paler blue, outlining and shading in blue-black. Her beak and feet are shaded in yellow mixed with a spot of red, and the details of her feathers can be added in brown or black. Paint her shawl in a fairly dark pink and pale blue, in a rough paisley pattern over a white background. Outline the shawl in brown or black.

Mrs Tiggy-winkle

Outline her clothes in dark brown or black, and add her prickles in dark brown through the cap. Her apron is creamy white (add a spot of yellow), and her iron is grey, held with a green cloth. Her fur is darker around her eye, which is black all round with a white centre, grey beneath.

To scale down the figures

Scaled down in size, these plaques make perfect name plates to stick on a bedroom door with a couple of self-adhesive pads.

From The Tale of Mrs. Tiggy-Winkle

Or you can drill a hole in the bottom of each plaque and attach it to the back of a door with a screw-in hook on which to hang up a dressing gown.

Scale down the outlines in the same way you enlarged them, but make your second grid half the size of the first rectangle.

124

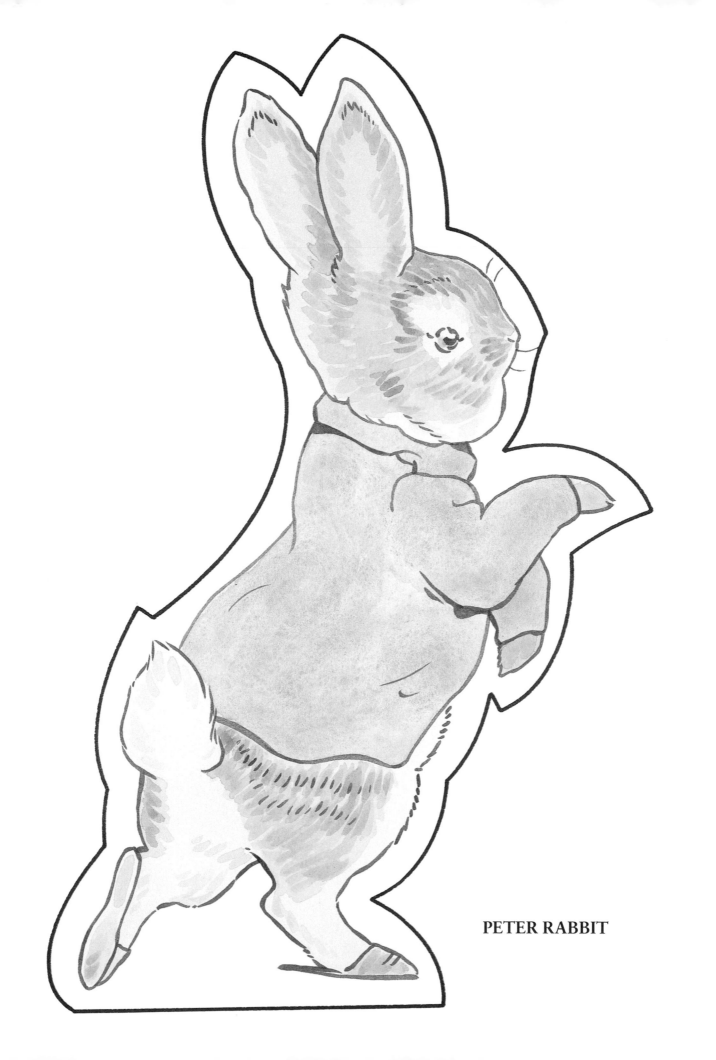

PETER RABBIT

BENJAMIN BUNNY

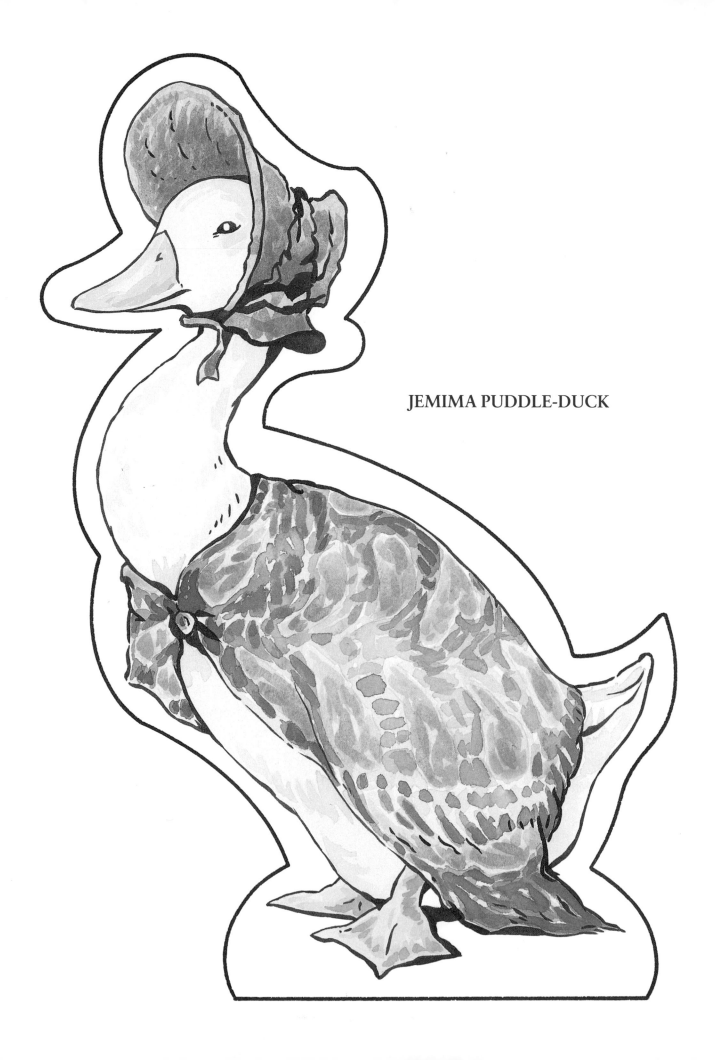

JEMIMA PUDDLE-DUCK

Pictures to cut out
for découpage overleaf